PREFACE.

A recent work by M. Guyau was originally announced under the title of *The Non-Religion of the Future*, and, doubtless, an impression is generally prevalent that, with the modification or disappearance of traditional forms of Belief, the fate of Religion itself is involved.

The present volume is a plea for a reconsideration of the Religious question, and an inquiry as to the possibility of reconstructing Religion by shifting its basis from inscrutable dogmas to the unquestionable facts of man's moral nature. It is now some fifty years since Emerson wrote that "the progress of Religion is steadily towards its identification with Morals," and foretold "a new Church founded on Moral Science . . . the Church of men to come". It is more than a century since the immortal Immanuel Kant startled Europe by the betrayal of the immensity of the emotion whereby the contemplation of "man's sense of law" filled his soul, shedding henceforth an unfading glory about the ideal of Duty and Virtue, and elevating it in the strictest sense to the supreme height of Religion. What these men—the prophet and philosopher of the New Idealism—thought and did has borne fruit in the foundation in America, Great Britain and Ireland, in France, Germany, Austria and Italy, of Centres or Societies of Ethical Culture which assume as axiomatic that there is, there can be, no Religion but that which makes us one with the Moral Progress of Humanity, by incessant co-operation with "the Power that makes for Righteousness". If

Religion be, what its name signifies, the unifying principle of mankind, in no other wise can we be possibly made One with each other and with the Universal Power than by so living as to secure the ends for which worlds and men exist. As the great Ethical prophet of the West expressed the truth: "My Father worketh even until now, and I also work". In such co-operation by moral life we place the very essence of Religion.

With a view to propagating such a conception of Religion, wholly based on Morality, a Society was founded in the autumn of the past year which assumed the title of "The Ethical Religion Society," and described itself as a branch of "The Ethical Church," "the Church of men to come," which is one day to emerge from the united efforts of all who believe in the everlasting "Sovereignty of Ethics," the unconditioned Supremacy of the Moral Law. The Ethical Movement is now beginning to spread in Europe and America. It is represented very largely in the United States, where, indeed, it was inaugurated some twenty years ago by Dr. Felix Adler, of New York; in Germany, by a score or more of Societies; in Italy, in Austria, in Hungary, and quite recently in France and Norway. London, of course, is represented by numerous Societies, and Ireland possesses one at Belfast. So far, there has been nothing definite accomplished towards a federation of these representative Bodies, though some preliminary steps have been taken in the formation of an international committee. The various Societies are quite independent, nor are their speculative opinions always in agreement. One only principle is universally and unreservedly acknowledged, namely, *the absolute supremacy and independence of Morality*, whatever philosophical differences may exist as to speculative matters connected therewith. The Movement stands for freedom. *In certis, unitas; in dubiis, libertas.*

As regards the Ethical Religion Society, which meets at Steinway Hall, Portman Square, and for which alone the present volume has any claim to speak, it may be said that it expresses the Ethical interpretation with which the teaching of Kant and Emerson, and the Idealist school generally, have made us familiar. During the year of its existence it may be said to have met a certain need, and to have gained numerous adherents from amongst those who, finding it impossible to "stand upon the old ways," were yet in need of an Idealism and an inspiration of life. The teaching given weekly at its Sunday Services is summarised in the following chapters, which are published under the impression that some information respecting a Body which is content to make the Moral life its ideal and reverence Conscience as "the highest, holiest" reality, may be welcome to religious idealists generally. The volume is altogether of an introductory character, and merely aims at conveying the central truth of Ethical Religion expressed by Immanuel Kant in the well-known words—*Religion is Morality recognised as a Divine command. Morality is the foundation. Religion only adds the new and commanding point of view.*

MORALITY AS A RELIGION.

I.

ETHICS AND RELIGION.

Some fifteen years ago a discussion was carried on in the pages of one of our leading monthlies on the profoundly important question, "The Influence on Morality of a Decline in Religious Belief". Men of every shade of opinion, from Roman Catholicism to Agnosticism, contributed their views, and, as might well have been expected, they came to the most contradictory conclusions. The Roman Catholic and Anglican writers appeared to think that the mere husk of morality would be left with the disappearance of Christianity; that a sort of enlightened epicureanism, a prudent animalism, would sway the greater part of mankind; in a word, that we should be "whited sepulchres," fair to look on without, but "inside full of dead men's bones, and all filthiness". The agnostic was no less certain that morality, which had outgrown the cumbrous garments manufactured by theology, would get on equally well in the handy raiment provided by science. The Rev. Dr. Martineau, speaking as a theistic philosopher, accurately delineated the boundaries of religion and morality, proceeded to show the untenableness of these two extreme positions, and nobly vindicated the complete autonomy or independence of ethics, whether of theological or scientific doctrines.

Before stating the views which an ethical society advocates as to the relations between religion and ethics, it would be very opportune to remark that in the symposium or discussion referred to, sufficient emphasis was not laid on an extremely important distinction which should be borne in mind when we estimate the comparative importance of religion and ethics. It is this. Religion, to ninety-nine out of every hundred men who talk about it, does not mean religion in its genuine character, but philosophy. A man's religion is merely a synonym for the reasoned explanation of the universe, of man, and their destiny, which he has learnt from the particular ecclesiastical organisation to which he belongs. Thus, the Christian religion means to the Anglican the Bible as interpreted by the Thirty-nine Articles; to the Dissenter, the same book, as interpreted by some confession, such as the Westminster, the Calvinistic, or the like. To the Roman Catholic it is synonymous with what has been, and what in future may be, the verdict of a central teaching corporation whose judgment is final and irrevocable. Similarly, religion for the Mohammedan is the precise form which his founder gave it, whilst the Buddhist is equally persistent in upholding the version of Sakya Mouni. Now, it is plain that religion itself is one definite thing, and cannot be made to cover a multiplicity of contradictory statements. What, then, are these Catholic, Protestant, Mohammedan and Buddhist religions? They are not religions at all: they are merely philosophies, or systematised accounts of God, the world, and of man, which have obtained large support in earlier stages of the world's history. Religion itself is a thing apart from these ephemeral forms in which it has been made to take shape. It is the great sun of reality, whose pure and authentic radiance has been decomposed in the spectrum of the human brain, each man seizing on an individual ray of broken light and making that the sum and substance of his belief.

 Our little systems have their day,
 They have their day and cease to be;

> They are but broken lights of Thee,
> And Thou, O Lord, art more than they.

It is the aim of this movement, for the establishment of ethical religion, to re-discover to man's wondering eyes the imperishable beauty of a religion allied to no transitory elements, wrapped up in no individual philosophy, bounded by no limitations of time, place or race, but ever the self-same immutable reality, though manifesting itself in most diverse ways, the sense of the infinite in man, and the communion of his spirit with that alone.

> Speak to Him, thou, for He hears, and spirit with spirit can meet,
> Closer is He than breathing, and nearer than hands or feet.

What has philosophy, creed or council to say to that high and ennobling conception? Shall "articles" and "confessions" venture to intrude there in the innermost sanctuary of man's spiritual being and dictate to him what he shall hold or not hold of a reality about which he alone is conscious? What has the conflict about the Hebrew cosmogony, of Genesis, baptismal regeneration, or the validity of orders to do with that serene peace in which religion alone can dwell? It were profanity surely to intrude such strife of words in a sanctuary so sacred as that.

One of our saddest thoughts as we reflect on the "little systems," so called, of the day, must be that they have so inconceivably belittled religion, tearing away that veil of reverence which should ever enshrine the Holy of Holies. The only atmosphere in which religion can really live is one of intense reverence, and when we hear of revivals, pilgrimages, elaborate ritualism (I am afraid Emerson describes it as "peacock ritual"), we may safely doubt whether the soul of religion be there. It is an excitement, a large advertisement for one or other of the many ecclesiastical corporations of the age, but where is the lonely communing with the Unseen, as revealed in the story of Jesus or the Buddha? The reason why Jesus is so fascinating a memory to his church disciples is that he is so wholly unlike them. So little is there really spiritual and suggestive of the higher life in what is exclusively ecclesiastical, that in their best moments men instinctively turn away from it, and find inspiration and peace in quiet thoughts about the Master, who said, "The Kingdom of God," that is the kingdom of righteousness, or the ethical church, "cometh not with observation," and "The Kingdom of God is within you". The more inward religion is, the less formalism it employs, the more ethical it becomes, the nearer it approaches the ideal of the great Master. A pure and saintly inspiration, an ennobling and yet subduing influence, a solemn stillness and hushing of the senses that would contend for mastery, an odour blown from "the everlasting hills," filling life with an indescribable fragrance; such is religion as professed and taught by Jesus, and such is the ideal of the Church of Emerson, builded on the purified emotions of the human heart.

Perhaps I have now indicated what I mean by religion, "pure and undefiled," though I know too well what truth lies hid in those words of the "Over-soul," "Ineffable is the union of man and God in every act of the soul". The spoken word does but suggest, and that faintly, what the inner word of the soul expresses on matters so sublime. Still, so far as the limitations of thought and speech permit, we have shown how religion is the communion of man's spirit with the "Over-soul," the baring of his heart before the immensities and eternities which encompass him, the deep and beautiful soliloquy of the soul in the silence of the Great Presence.

> Draw, if thou canst, the mystic line
> Severing rightly His from thine,
> Which is human, which Divine.
> —*Conduct of Life*.

Let us now pass on to inquire what are the relations between religion so conceived and ethics or morality. In the first place, it must be laid down as clearly as words will permit that religion and morality should always be conceived as separate realities. Of course, there can be no such thing as religion "pure and undefiled" without morality or right conduct; nevertheless, the two words connote totally distinct activities of the soul of man. We shall best explain our meaning by pointing to the obvious fact that there have not been wanting men in all times who have exhibited an almost ideal devotion to duty without betraying any sympathy whatsoever with religious emotion such as has been described. They have no sense of the infinite, as others have no sense of colour, art or music, and in nowise feel the need of that transcendent world wherein the object of religion is enshrined. I should say that the elder Mill was such a man, and his son, John Stuart Mill, until the latter years of his life, when his views appear to have undergone a marked change. Some of his disappointed friends ascribed the change to the serious shock he suffered at his wife's death. There may possibly be truth in that opinion; "the winnowing wings of death" often bring about a searching change. No one yet has ever been able to seriously live up to the Hedonistic rule, "eat and drink for to-morrow we die". If death were announced, the very last thing man would do would be to eat and make merry.

However, it is notoriously possible to "bring forth fruits of righteousness," or, to use modern language, to live the good life, without seeking any help from that world of the ideal in which religion lives. This teaching, of course, is diametrically opposed to that of the Churches, who lay it down almost as an axiom that without such extraneous assistance as "grace," generally conveyed in answer to direct supplication, or through the mystery of Sacramental agencies, such as Baptism or the Lord's Supper, it is fairly impossible to keep the moral law. To the credit of humanity, this dark theology has been falsified by results in countless instances, and never more frequently than to-day. Men whose names are in the mouth of everybody have lived and died in the enjoyment not merely of the esteem, but of the reverent admiration of their age, whose lives were wholly uninspired by religious motives. I need only mention Charles Darwin, and when we remember that not even sectarianism ventured to dispute his right to rest within the hallowed precincts of an abbey-cathedral, ecclesiastics themselves must be fast forgetting the deplorable narrowness of old views which made morality and dogmatism inter-dependent terms.

Nevertheless, it must be conceded, and such men as I have spoken of were the first to admit it, that lives such as these are necessarily imperfect. The stunting or the atrophy of the religious instinct, the hunger and thirst for something beyond the sphere of sense when left totally unsatisfied, produces at length a restless, tormented feeling, which turns the very joy of existence to sadness, and dims the light of life. Such men may plunge into pleasure, absorb themselves in their books or research, wear and waste themselves in the making of wealth, and for a time they are satisfied. But the imperious craving reasserts itself at length; there is the cry of the soul for some lost inspiration, some transfiguring influence to soften the hard way of life, console a lonely hour, comfort a bereavement, inspire that tenderness and sympathy, without which we are scarcely even human. One remembers Darwin's sorrowful admission, that the deadening of his spiritual instincts left him incapable of enjoying, or even tolerating, the rhythm of the poet's verse. The world has heard the note of weariness with which Mr. Spencer absolved himself from further effort on behalf of science and man. The late Prof. Romanes, in his volume entitled *A Candid Examination of Theism*, made the melancholy declaration that the admission of a philosophy of pure mechanism or materialism had, for him at least, "robbed the universe of its soul of beauty". In later years, as is well known, the same writer came to see things with other eyes. Mind took the place of force as the ultimate fact of creation, and with it the sun of loveliness returned once more.

Have we ever sufficiently reflected that the purely negative philosophy has done nothing for idealism in any shape or form? It has inspired no art, music or poetry. With nothing to draw upon but the blind whirl of infinite atoms and infinite forces, of which man is himself the haphazard and highest production, it has contented itself with the elementary work of destruction, without even attempting to dig the foundations for anything which it is proposed to erect in the place of what has been destroyed. "Scepticism," says Carlyle, "is, after all, only half a magician. She calls up more spectres than she can lay." Scepticism was, nay is, sometimes, a necessary attitude of the human mind. But man cannot live on doubt alone, and therefore, though we profoundly believe the possibility of living the good life independently of religious sanctions, we unhesitatingly affirm the deep need man has of religious emotion to satisfy the ineradicable instinct of his nature towards communion with the unseen world. Here are the words of a man who had exhausted the possibilities of life before he wrote them, conveying in the simplest, though most penetrating way, a most momentous truth: "*Fecisti nos Domine ad Te, et irrequiêtum est cor nostrum donec requiescat in Te*". "*Thou hast made us, O Lord, for Thyself, and our heart is restless until it find rest in Thee*." And if we would have a modern commentary upon this saying of the fourth century writer, Augustine of Hippo, here are a few words of Victor Hugo, spoken in the French Parliament of the forties: "*Dieu se retrouve à la fin de tout*".

Before leaving this point, it would be well to complete the argument by distinctly stating that, as morality is possible without religion, religion—or rather we should call it religiosity—is possible without morality. This is a matter of very great importance, and what has been asserted will help us to understand the curious phenomena one meets with in all periods of the world's history—men and women, apparently of undeniable religious instincts, exhibiting a most imperfect appreciation of the far more weighty matters concerned with moral conduct. I am not speaking of downright hypocrites who make religion merely a cloak for the realisation of rascally designs. I speak rather of such individuals, who, while betraying a marked religious fervour, showing itself in assiduous attention at church services, proselytising, and religious propaganda generally, manifest on the other hand little or no delicacy or sensitiveness of conscience on purely ethical matters. Take for example such men as Torquemada and the inquisitors, or Calvin amongst the Protestants; take the orgies of sensuality which were the necessary accompaniment of much religious worship in Pagan times, and, if we may believe travellers, are not wholly dissociated with popular religion in India and China to-day. Or, again, take such a case as that of the directors of the Liberator Building Society, men whose prospectuses, annual reports, and even announcements of dividends, were saturated with the unction of religious fervour. Or, take the tradesman who may be a churchwarden or deacon at his church or chapel, but exhibits no scruples whatever in employing false weights, and, worst of all, in adulterating human food. An incalculable amount of this sort of thing goes on, and, whether it be accurate or not I cannot say, it is often ascribed to small dealers in small towns and villages, "pillars of the church," as a rule, which they may happen to attend.

Now, in all these cases there is no need to suppose conscious hypocrisy. Unconscious, possibly; but, though the heart of man be inscrutable, we need not necessarily believe that such phenomena are open evidence of wilful self-deceit. The far truer explanation is, that religious emotion is one thing and moral emotion quite another. The late chairman of the Liberator Building Company, I can well conceive, was a fervent and devoted adherent of his sect, and was not consciously insincere, when, in paying dividends out of capital, he ascribed his prosperity to the unique care of a heavenly providence which especially occupied itself about all he personally undertook. The rascality of Saturday was entirely forgotten on Sunday, when, with bowed head, he recited his metaphysical creed or received the parting blessing. The Sunday service, the surpliced choir, those melting hymns, the roll of the organ's mysterious tones throughout the holy edifice, the peculiar sense of spiritual well-being and prosperity which it all combined to produce was probably a joy of his life, and by no means the meanest. The mischief was that he had no moral sense, and the word honesty and duty connoted nothing real to his mis-shapen mind. He was a morally deficient being.

Now, the ethical Church has come for this great purpose, to make us see the repulsiveness of a religion of that kind, to assure every man that no religious services, any more than the eager subscription of antiquated formularies, constitute the essence of religion. That is built on the moral law, and unless it come as the crown and glory of a life of duty, then that religion is a shameful thing, the sacrilegious degradation of the highest and holiest thing on earth. It has come, this ethical Church, to reinforce the wholly forgotten teaching of the Hebrew prophets of the utter emptiness of all religion devoid of moral life, the vanity of sacrifices, oblations and rites, the hollowness of formularies, creeds and confessions, the indispensable necessity of an ethical basis for all religious belief and practice. "What more," asks Micah, "doth the Lord require of thee than to do justice, love mercy, and to walk humbly with thy God?"

It has come also to indicate the true relations between ethics and religion. Ethics are truly the basis on which religion is built, but when once the sacred edifice is fully raised, a beautiful reaction is set up (at least in the ideal good life), and religion becomes one of the strongest incentives to a dutiful and virtuous life. This is the explanation of the truly ideal lives lived by men and women of deep personal religion, in all sects and creeds,

European and Asiatic. This, too, is the justification of that oft-repeated and profoundly true saying, that all good men and women belong to the same religion. It is to that one true, pure, and aboriginal religion we wish to get back, in which we discover the best ally of morality, the all-powerful incentive to a life wholly devoted to duty and the service of the human brotherhood. The allegory of the Last Judgment, as it is called, as depicted by Jesus himself in the Gospel according to Matthew, emphasises this ethical truth in words of great solemnity. The sheep and the goats are distinguished, not by the possession or non-possession of miraculous spiritual powers, professions of belief or Church membership, but by the humble devotion exhibited to suffering humanity, and steadfast perseverance in the path of duty. How was it possible, we ask again and again, for such a religion as that to be transformed into the thing of shreds and patches of bad philosophy as set forth in the Nicene and Athanasian Creed?

Forget all that, we would fain exhort men, forget all but the words that made music on the Galilean hills, the life "lived in the loveliness of perfect deeds," the veritable exemplar of a religion founded on the moral sentiment. To be touched by the influence of religious emotion is to approach in greater or less degree to the image and character of Christ. To live a life of devotion to duty, however humble our station may be, is to range ourselves, with that great Master of ethics, on the side of an eternal order of righteousness which can never fail. It is to work with that soul of reason dominating everything in the animate and inanimate world, to co-operate with it towards the fulfilment of those high ends which are predestined for humanity. Every man must make his choice. Either he will ally himself with all that makes for moral advancement—his own, that of others, and consequently of the world—or he will fight for the powers of retrogression and decay. He will live for the hour and its momentary pleasures, fight for his own hand alone, forget mercy and pity, seldom think, never reflect, and at length, sated and yet dissatisfied with all he has experienced, sink impotently and ignobly into the grave. Immanuel Kant lays it down as an axiom that the moral law must inevitably be fulfilled one day in every individual human being. It is the destiny of man to be one day perfect. What a searching change must sometime pass over those who have taken the wrong side in this earth-life, who have helped on the process of disintegration, and contrived to leave the world worse than they found it! They fight for a losing cause: they lose themselves in fighting for it.

It has been said, I have heard it said myself, that "ethics are cold". Possibly to some they are; but at any rate they are grave and solemn when they hold language such as this to the pleasure-loving, the light-hearted, and the indifferent. To tell a man to do his duty in spite of all, to love the good life irrespectively of any reward here or hereafter, may sound cold after the dithyrambics of the Apocalypse or the Koran, but of one thing we are assured by the experience of those who have made the trial of it themselves, that any man who "will do the doctrine," that is, live the life, shall know at once "whether it be of God"—that alone is the unspeakable peace, passing all understanding.

But ethics are not alone. As I have endeavoured to point out, religious emotion which grows out of the moral sentiment is the most powerful stimulus towards the realisation of the good life, and I consequently urged the supreme value of true religion, as both satisfying the emotional side of man's nature and stimulating him towards that sacrifice of self—that taking up of a "cross," as Jesus put it—which in some measure is indispensably necessary for the attainment of character.

But I in no wise concede that ethics are "cold"; I in no wise admit they are uninspiring. The consciousness that a man possesses of being one with the great Power of the universe in making for righteousness is surely an overwhelming thought. If man would but think, he would come to feel with Emerson "the sublimity of the moral laws," their awful manifestation of the working of infinite mind and power, and of man's nearness to, or rather oneness with, that Power, when he obeys them. He would come to thrill with an indescribable emotion with Kant, as he thinks of the infinite dignity to which fellowship with those mysterious laws elevates him. He would realise the truth of the solemn words:—

> Two things fill me with ceaseless awe,
> The starry heavens, and man's sense of law.

Ethics cold! Then what else is left to inspire to us? We are bankrupt. What is there in all the Churches to help humanity if not their ethics—ethics which are not the perquisite of any sect, no mere provincialism of any Church or nation, but the heirloom of mankind?

What, we ask, is there to cheer the heart in the Thirty-nine Articles, the Vatican decrees, or the Westminster Confession? What mysterious inspiration lurks in the dogmas of the Oriental councils of 1600 years ago, dogmas to be believed to-day under peril of perishing everlastingly? We do not concede that the ethical Church has no message to the heart, no comfort for the emotions, no solace to the deeply tried and afflicted. A Church which preaches the imperishability of every good deed, the final and decisive victory of the good; which reveals to us not only mind, but beneficence, as the character of the supreme Power in the universe; which bids us remember that as that Power is, so are we, moral beings to our heart's core, and, in consequence, to take the place which belongs to us at the side of the infinite righteousness for the furtherance of the good—such a Church, such a religion is not destitute of enthusiasm and inspiration. A philosophy such as this, a religion such as this, will one day sweep the English-speaking countries in a tempest of enthusiasm. It will be welcomed as the final settlement of the conflicting claims of mind and heart in man, the reconciliation of the feud too long existing between religion and science. Everything points to its immense future. Within the churches its principles are tacitly accepted as irrefutable. We claim such men as Stanley, Maurice and Jowett as preachers of the ethical Church, and their numbers are increasing every year among the cultured members of the Anglican clergy. Leading men of science are no longer committed to a purely negative philosophy, while one and all would be prepared to admit that if religion we are to have it must be one in complete harmony with the moral sentiment in the best men; in other words, a Church founded on moral science, the ideal of the saintly Jesus, and of all the prophets of the race.

NOTE.—"I can conceive the existence of a Church in which, week by week, services should be devoted, not to the iteration of abstract propositions in theology, but to the setting before men's minds of an ideal of true, just and pure living: a place in which those who are weary of the burden of daily cares should find a moment's rest in the contemplation of the higher life which is possible for all, though attained by so few; a place in which the man of strife and of business should have time to think how small after all are the rewards he covets compared with peace and charity. *Depend upon it, if such a Church existed, no one would seek to disestablish it.*"—HUXLEY. I know not what better words could be chosen wherewith to describe the ethical Church.

II

ETHICS AND SCIENCE.

Since the era of the re-birth of learning, each successive century has been generally distinguishable by some marked intellectual development, by some strong movement which has taken deep hold of the minds of men. Thus the Renascimento period was followed by the century of the Reformation, and that again by the inauguration of the era of modern philosophy, while the eighteenth century has been claimed as the *Saeculum Rationalisticum*, the age of rationalism, in which the claims of reason were pushed to the forefront in the domains of religion and politics. Nothing remained after that but an age of physical science, and surely enough has been given us in the nineteenth century which may with equal accuracy be termed the *Saeculum Scientificum*.

It cannot be doubted that a sort of mental intoxication has been set up as a result of the extraordinary successes which have rewarded the efforts of scientific investigators. Everything now-a-days is expressed in terms of science and its formulae. Evolution is the keynote to the learning of the age. Thus Mr. Spencer's system of the Synthetic Philosophy is a bold and comprehensive attempt to take up the whole knowable, and express it anew in the language of development. It is emphatically, professedly, the philosophy of evolution, the rigid application of a purely scientific formula to everything capable of philosophical treatment. Now, having discussed the question of ethics and religion, their distinction and their intimate relations; having shown how that religion comes as the crown and glory of the ethical life, the transfiguration of the ethical ideal and the most powerful stimulus towards the realisation in practice of what is conceived as theoretically desirable, it remains for us to complete our treatment of this aspect of the ethical problem and determine the relations existing between morals and science.

This question we conceive to be of vital importance. Just as we must be inexorable in refusing to base our ethic on religion, and still less on theology, so must we be equally determined in repudiating the claim often put forward, that morality is a department of physics, or in any way founded on physical science. The scientific professor, feeling the ground strong under his feet, and sure of the applause of his very numerous public, has made a bold bid for the control of the moral order. He has made a serious attempt to capture the ethical world, and to coerce morality into obedience to the inflexible formulae of physics. The evolutionist, in particular, is consumed with an irresistible desire to stretch the ethical ideal on his procrustean couch and to show how, like everything else, it has been the subject of painfully slow growth and development, and that when the stages of that growth have been accurately ascertained by research into the records of the past, the essence of morality is fully explained. Originally non-extant, it has become at length, after aeons of struggle, the chief concern of man, the "business of all men in common," as Locke puts it, all of which philosophy is tantamount to saying, that morality is merely a flatter of history. When you know its history, you know everything, very much as a photographer might claim to exhaustively know an individual man, because he had photographed him every six months from his cradle to his grave. A very inadequate philosophy of ethic, this.

But, before coming to close quarters with this extremely interesting problem, I would protest that we are sincere in our loyalty and enthusiasm for physical science, sincere in our deep admiration for its chief exponents. We claim to be students of the students of nature, for, after all, nature herself is the great scientist. The secrets are all in her keeping. The All-Mother is venerable indeed in the eyes of every one of us. "The heated pulpiteer" may denounce modern science as the evil genius of our day, the arch-snare of Satan for the seduction of unwary souls and the overthrow of Biblical infallibility, but we are not in that galley. As true sons of our age, we are loyal to its spirit, and that spirit is scientific. The late Professor Tyndall said of Emerson, the veritable prophet and inspiration of ethical religion: "In him we have a poet and a profoundly religious man, who is really and entirely undaunted by the discoveries of science, past, present and prospective, and in his case poetry, with the joy of a bacchanal, takes her graver brother science by the hand, and cheers him with immortal laughter. By Emerson scientific conceptions are continually transmuted into the finer forms and warmer lines of an ideal world." It is in no spirit, therefore, of hostility to physical science or her methods that we venture to point out that the term science is not synonymous with experimental research. The most brilliant work of Darwin, Kelvin or Edison in no wise alters the fact that there are more things in heaven and earth than are revealed by their microscopes or decomposed in their crucibles. Mental science, and above all moral or ethical science, have a claim to be heard as well as physics. Philosophy, strictly speaking, working by the light, not of the senses, as does physical science, but by the higher light of the intelligence alone, must be reckoned with by the thoughtful man. Yet this is precisely what so many of the lesser luminaries of science, the popul03arisers of the great discoveries made by other and greater men, appear to be wholly unable to see. They have borrowed their foot-rule for the mensuration of the universe, and they apply it indiscriminately. Everything, from the dead earth to the glowing inspiration of the prophet's soul, must be labelled in terms of that infallible instrument. If it cannot be reduced to their exiguous standard, so much the worse for it. Science, or rather "the heated pulpiteer" of science (for these inflammatory gentlemen are found both in the pulpit and at the rostrum), can take no account of it, and that settles the matter once for all.

We may proceed to offer a few illustrations of the attempt of the scientist to capture the domain of ethics. The late Professor Huxley, of whom we would speak with all the respect due to his high position as a scientific expositor, roundly asserts that "the safety of morality is in the keeping of science," meaning, of course, physical science. The same authority considers science a far "better guardian of morality than the pair of old shrews, philosophy and theology," in whose keeping he evidently thinks everybody, not a scientist, believes morality to rest. The teaching of such men as Mr. Spencer, Mr. Bain, and Mr. Leslie Stephen, though they lack the vigour and picturesqueness of Mr. Huxley's unique style, comes to much the same thing. Under the extraordinary delusion that all the world, excepting a few enlightened scientific men, believes morality to be under the tutelage of a "pair of shrews," to wit, philosophy and theology, they at once proceed to fly to the opposite extreme error, and to proclaim that it is under the guardianship of physical science. We have already satisfied ourselves that morality is not based on religion, but contrariwise that religion is built on the sanctified emotions of the human heart, that is on the moral ideal—"a new church founded on moral science"—and as to theology, I should not waste my time in attempting to show that morality is not based on that. But it will be worth our while to show that Mr. Huxley and his brethren are under a serious misapprehension when they suppose that having dispossessed theology of a property which no sane man believes it ever possessed, they are at once entitled to appropriate the same themselves in the name of physical science. We shall see that there is a third claimant in the field of whom the extremists on either side appear to have lost sight, and that when the case is fully set forth a verdict in its favour will be inevitable. Meanwhile, let us look at the scientific claim. Is the criterion of conduct in the custody of the scientific experimenter? If a man wanted to know whether a certain act was good, bad or indifferent, such a course of conduct permissible or not, is he to consult the biologist or the chemist?

I venture to affirm, in language of the most explicitness, that physical science can know absolutely nothing about morality; that ethics are a matter of profound indifference to it, that, as Diderot, the encyclopaedist—certainly not suspect in such matters—says, "To science there can be no question of the unclean or the unchaste". You might as well ask a physician for an opinion about law as to put a case of conscience before an astronomer.

There has been, as a matter of fact, an extraordinary amount of loose thinking concerning the precise relations between science, ethics and religion. The churches, having become irretrievably discredited in their doctrinal teaching (their very ministers, in the persons of Stanley and Jowett, openly avowing disbelief in their articles and creeds), religion has come to be looked upon as a sort of no man's land, and therefore the legitimate property of the first occupier. Science, as the enterprising agency *par excellence* of the century, has stepped in, and in claiming to exhaustively explain religion, virtually claims to have simultaneously annexed morality, erroneously looked upon as a department of religion.

But a little more careful thinking ought to convince the most eager of the advance-agents of physical science that the discipline they serve so loyally is altogether unconcerned with the moral life, and wholly incompetent to deal with its problems. Mr. Frederic Harrison once asked, and with extreme pertinence, what the mere dissector of frogs could claim to know of the facts of morality and religion? Positively nothing, *as such*, and in their more sober moments "the beaters of the drum" scientific would appear to be well aware of the fact. For instance, Mr. Huxley himself, oblivious of all he had claimed in the name of physical science, asked with surprise, in what laboratory questions of aesthetics and historical truth could be tested? In what, indeed? we may well ask. And yet the physical science which is avowedly incapable of deciding the comparatively insignificant matters of taste and history is prepared to take over with the lightest of hearts the immense burden of morality and to become the conscience-keeper, I had almost said the Father Confessor, of humanity! I imagine Mr. Huxley himself would have shrunk before the assumption of such responsibility.

But let us approach the matter more closely. To physical science, one act is precisely the same as another; a mere matter of molecular movement or change. You raise your arm, you think with the energy and profundity of a Hegel; to the physicist it is all one and the same thing—a fresh distribution of matter and motion, muscular contraction, and rise and fall of the grey pulp called brain. A burglar shoots a policeman dead and the public headsman decapitates a criminal. To physical science, those two acts differ in no respect. They are exercises of muscular energy, expenditure of nervous power, the effecting of molecular change, and there the matter ends. But surely, you would urge, the scientist would discriminate between those two acts. Most assuredly. The one he would reprobate as immoral, and the other he would approve as lawful. But, be it carefully noted, he would do this, not as a scientist, but as a citizen respecting law and order and upholding good government based on morality and justice. As a moralist, then, but not as a scientist does he pass judgment, for there is no experimental science which deals with such matters. Physics concerns itself solely with what it can see and handle—nothing else. The actions, therefore, of right and wrong, justice and injustice, morality and immorality are simply unintelligible to it, just as unintelligible as they are to the most highly developed animal. It is the fully developed mind or intelligence alone which apprehends the sublime conception of duty, and the indefeasible claims which it has upon the allegiance of the will, and, in consequence, the scientist who denounces injustice and iniquity is no longer on the tripod of the professor, but in the rostrum of the ethical teacher. If I may say so, it supplies us with an admirable illustration of a quick-change performance. The same man performs a double part, and so adroitly is the change managed, that the performer himself is deceived into thinking that he is still the scientist, whereas he has become for the moment the moral professor. But he did not acquire that new teaching in the laboratory; he learnt it in the study.

But there is distinctly one point of close contact between science and morality, which we must not omit to point out. Physical science, particularly physiology, from its intimate acquaintance with the human organism, is admirably adapted for the function of a danger-signal, so to speak, to warn the ignorant and indifferent that a life undisciplined and ill-regulated cannot but end in irretrievable disaster. It thus most powerfully subserves the ends of private and individual morality, just as historical science, which, as Professor Huxley accurately noted, can in no wise be tested in a retort or a crucible, can point the moral when the lawless actions of public bodies or nations threaten the foundations upon which society rests. The physiologist can preach a sermon of appalling severity to the drunkard; he can describe internal and external horrors (as certain to ensue in the victim's case, as night follows day), compared with which the imaginings of a Dante are comparatively tame. He can likewise depict a deplorable future of disease and decay as reserved for the vicious. He can point to a veritable Gehenna strewn with the corpses of unnumbered victims. He can prove to demonstration, if we listen to him, that no organisation such as ours can resist the awful strain put upon it by the poison of alcohol, and the enervating results of an undisciplined existence.

"Reform," he can tell us, "or go to perdition;" and most valuable his sermon will be.

Would that men, so favourably endowed with this intimate knowledge of the intricacy of the workings of our bodily frame, so utilised their great powers in the service of ethics, pointing out to the reckless transgressor what a scourge nature has in store for him, what indescribable disasters he is preparing for himself by his audacity in venturing to break her holy laws. In the Church which is to be, "the Church of men to come," the scientist will fill this very *rôle*. As the best interpreter of nature, he will be most fitly chosen to discourse to us of nature's laws. The priests of humanity in days to be will not be consecrated by a magical transmission of imaginary powers, but by their ascertained capacity to open a door in heaven and earth and reveal to us the secret workings of the Soul of the World. We shall meet in united worship in the great cathedrals, but no more to repeat the dead formulae of a past which is gone, but to hear the living word of to-day, the last revelation the Supreme has made, be it through the mouth of poet, prophet, philosopher or scientist. Then, and only then, shall the Catholic or Universal Church be born, "coming down out of heaven from God," visibly embracing all humanity, because excluding none prepared to subscribe the aboriginal creed of the supremacy of ethic, the everlasting sovereignty of the moral law.

But while we candidly acknowledge the priceless services which science can render to morality in the way indicated, this in no way warrants our assenting to Mr. Huxley's dictum that science is the guardian of morality. As a matter of fact, science points at the deplorable results of excess without any regard to morality whatsoever. She announces them as definite facts, as certain as to-morrow's sunrise, because she is intimately acquainted with the human organisation and the laws which control it. But she ventures on no opinion as to the moral worth of the acts in question; she registers results and there her work ends. If the scientist does happily go farther, and point out that conduct conducing to such disastrous consequences must be irredeemably bad in itself, he is doing most praiseworthy work, but he is no longer the scientist. He has slipped off his tripod, and is repeating the lesson of the moralist. Let us suppose the acts in question were not followed by unfortunate results. Say, for example, that by uttering a falsehood, by altering a figure in a will, or on a draft, one could inherit a fortune, what physical science could prevent our doing so, or instruct us as to the honesty or dishonesty of the contemplated action? Put thus, we see at a glance that the matter is outside the province of science, and quite beyond its jurisdiction. Morality, therefore, so far from being in the custody of science, has nothing whatsoever to do with it, but belongs to an entirely different order, and is ascertained by totally different methods.

If one would know the origin of the theory we are at present freely criticising, it can be indicated in a moment. The most ordinary induction has satisfied men that, in the long run, the Hebrew singer is right when he says, "The way of transgressors is hard". Wrong-doing and calamity are inseparably connected. Those laws, through which the voice of the Supreme is ever heard, are so intertwined in their action, that the infraction of one leads to the infliction of retributive punishment by the other. We break a moral law, the physical law will take up its cause, and we suffer. We have come, I say, to see the universal validity of this rule, the absolute irresistibility of the laws under which we live. Hence, a shallow judgment has been hastily framed that you may always judge of the morality of an act by the consequences it produces. If the results are good, then the action is good; if evil, then the action is adjudged bad. This is, in substance, the Benthamite or utilitarian ethic, Bentham roundly maintaining that crime is nothing but a miscalculation, an error in arithmetic. It is the failure of a man to count the cost, to weigh the results of what he is about to do. That being the case, the scientist being persuaded that utility and pleasure make an action good, and uselessness and pain make it bad, he was able to conclude at a stroke that one action differs only from another in the results it produces, and that since science was admirably equipped to take stock of results through its statistical bureau, she, and not the hideous old shrews, theology and philosophy, was the rightful protectress of morality.

But we, who believe with Immanuel Kant, that the "*All's well that ends well theory*" has no place in morality, refuse to recognise that the character of an action is determined solely by the results it produces. We believe that some actions are intrinsically good, and others intrinsically bad, totally irrespective of the good or evil they may effect. We believe with the Stoics and with Jesus that evil may be consummated in the heart without any evil results appearing at all. We believe that thoughts of envy, hatred, malice, are in themselves bad, irrespective of results, that such a thing as slander is *ipso facto* stamped as irredeemably bad long before any of its evil consequences may be manifest. We look not so much to consequence, but to the intention of the doer, and the intrinsic nature of the action performed. Pleasure and pain considerations are the last things we take into account when we weigh an action in the scales of justice. The theory is therefore hopelessly inadequate to our needs; it breaks in our hands when we attempt to use it, and, consequently, we refuse our assent to the proposition that because science can *occasionally* predict results she is therefore entitled to patronise ethics.

The truth is, that ethics need no such patronage. Neither the theologian nor the scientist is essential to their well-being. Ethics are beholden to neither of the two claimants who dispute the honour of their parentage and protection. They rest on that alone on which everything in this miraculous universe, science itself included, ultimately rests, the *reason* which is at the heart of things. The moral law, the sanction of the eternal distinction between right and wrong, a distinction valid before the very whisperings of science, aye, and of the voice of men were heard upon this earth, is, to the stately and impressive system of Emerson and Kant, the first-born of the eternal Reason itself, the very apprehensible nature of the Most High, which, the more men grow in the moral life, the more they recognise for his inner-most character and nature. Things are what they are, and actions are what they are, not because of the ephemeral judgments of a tribe or nation of men, but because they cannot be otherwise than they are, good or bad in themselves, judged solely by reference to that everlasting law of righteousness, the aboriginal enactment of the Eternal.

Men point to the growth and development of the moral sentiment in man, they show how he has grown from savagery to civilisation, and think therein that they have explained everything. They are like the photographer I spoke of above. They have found out the history of ethics, and they think there is nothing more to know. Far from it. Identically the same might be said of music and logic. Man once beat a tom-tom, and now he writes operas and oratorios. He once rambled, now he reasons. Will any sane man delude himself into believing that music and logic are nothing more in themselves but the history of the successive stages through which they have naturally and inevitably passed? Neither then is ethic and the moral law. It is not man's creation, it is not his handiwork. It is no mere provincialism of this dwindling sphere of ours, but a fact and a law supreme, holding sway beyond the uttermost star, valid in infinity and eternity, at this hour, the sovereign law of life for whatsoever or whomsoever lives and knows, the adamantine foundation upon which all law, civilisation, religion and progress are built.

"This is," says Burke in his magnificent language, "that great immutable pre-existent law, prior to our devices, and prior to all our sensations, antecedent to our very existence, by which we are knit and connected in the eternal frame of the universe, out of which we cannot stir." And not only

Burke, but centuries before him, the great Roman orator, in language equally sublime, professed his enthusiastic belief in that same law, which "no nation can overthrow or annul; neither a senate nor a whole people can relieve us from its injunctions. It is the same in Athens and in Rome, the same yesterday, to-day, and for ever."

III.

ETHICS AND THEISM.

In the present chapter we propose to discuss the gravest of all the grave problems which gather round the central conception of ethic as the basis of religion. There are, it may be said, two great schools which hold respectively the doctrines which may be not unfitly described as the significance and the insignificance, or rather, non-significance of ethics. The latter school, which is that of Bentham, Mill and Spencer, is content to take ethic as a set of formulae of utility which man has, in the course of his varied experience, discovered to be serviceable guides of life. There is no binding force in them; the idea of a conscience "trembling like a guilty thing surprised" because it has broken one of these laws, the hot flush of shame which seems to redden the very soul at the sense of guilt, the agony of remorse so powerful as sometimes to send the criminal self-confessed and self-condemned to his doom, is all said to be part of an obsolete form of speculation. There is merely "a *feeling* of obligation," such as an animal may experience which is harnessed to a waggon or a load, but any real obligation, authoritatively binding on the conscience of man, is repudiated in terms.

Now this teaching I venture to describe as the insignificant ethic, the ethic which connotes nothing beyond the "feeling of obligation," and refuses to recognise in morality anything but a series of hints casually picked up, as to how mankind should behave in order to score in the game of life.

The significant ethic, on the other hand, discerns in the law of morality the pathway into the transcendental world, the realm of reason beyond the boundaries of the sense. It sees in morality the basis of religion; it discovers the fact of man's freedom to conform or not to conform to the eternal law; it unveils the reality of life beyond this earth-stage of existence, and last and chiefest of all, it discerns, in the words of Immanuel Kant, "a natural idea of pure theism" in the unmistakable reality of the moral law, from the very obvious fact that laws do not make themselves, but are enactments of reason or intelligence.

We propose, therefore, to address ourselves to the fundamental question—the question of questions—the being of a subsistent intelligence and a supreme moral will, responsible for man and all things, whom we in our own tongue name God, though it were more reverent to think and speak of the awful truth with Emerson, as the "Nameless Thought, the Super-personal Heart". We are to treat of theism, the philosophical, *not the theological*, term to designate the truth that the universe owes its existence to infinite Power and infinite Mind, and that morality is a fact because that Power is moral also. To quote Whittier's well-known lines, which express the essential truth of theism in words of exceeding simplicity combined with philosophic depth:—

   By all that He requires of me
 I know what He Himself must be;

or, to quote the more vigorous, but equally common-sense statement of the facts by Carlyle: "It was flatly inconceivable to him (Frederick the Great) that moral emotion could have been put into him by an entity which had none of its own". And finally, we propose to speak of theism, thus defined, in its relations to ethics or moral science, the discipline which treats of human conduct and its conformity with a recognised law of life, the systematising of those principles of life which man has learned by reason and experience during the course of his sojourn in this sphere of existence.

Let us begin by some attempt at a definition of our terms. Ethics, I take it, we are agreed to consider as the science concerned with conduct; that is, with the actions of man in so far as they conform or do not conform with a standard of right, whatever that standard may be. Ethical, moral, morally good, right, we take to be synonymous terms. The word metaphysical *male olet*, no doubt. It is unpalatable, and is suggestive of, if not synonymous with, the unreal. However, I do not think we need be concerned now with the repute or disrepute of metaphysic generally, since we all are agreed that theism, or that reality for which theism stands, is in the super-sensible, super-experiential world, and therefore if theism is an implication of ethics at all, it is, of course, a metaphysical one. As to theism itself, things are not quite so clear, for the term covers, or may be made to cover, a number of philosophic systems which are not in harmony with one another. Thus the theism of the Hebrew Scriptures would possibly be atheism to Hegel, while the great idealist's position might be pantheism or worse to a High Church curate. To us theism means that at the ground of being, at the heart of existence, there is a self-subsistent reality which we call by the highest name we know, *viz.*, reason or mind. "Before the chaos that preceded the birth of the heavens and the earth one only being existed, immense, silent, immovable, yet incessantly active; that being is the mother of the universe. I know not how this being is named, but I designate it by the word 'reason'." [1] Absolute, unconditioned intelligence is the *Theos* we acknowledge. This is the formulary of our philosophical creed, and as Luther fastened his forty theses to the doors of the Würtemburg Cathedral, I affix my two humble propositions to the postern of the ethical church, namely, first, that "In the beginning was Mind," and next, that the moral law is the highest expression of that Mind. And, moreover, that as the mind in man is so ordered as to naturally proceed from the more known to the less known, from the ascertained fact of the moral law, we ascend to the source of the moral law, which, like all things, takes its rise in the *apeiron*, the Boundless of Anaximander, the Infinite of Mr. Spencer. Theism, then, as thus explained, one discerns as an implication of the indisputable fact of morality, of the sovereignty of ethic, of the indestructible supremacy of conscience.

And here one may be allowed to quote a singularly luminous passage from the *Cours d'Histoire de la Philosophic Morale en 18ème Siècle* of Victor Cousin, p. 318. "Kant remarks at this point," he says, "that we have no right to derive our moral ideas from the idea of God, because it is precisely from the moral ideas themselves that we are led to recognise a Supreme Being, the personification of absolute righteousness. Consequently, no-one may look upon the laws of morality as arbitrary enactments of the will of God. Virtue is not obligatory from the sole reason that it is a Divine ordinance; on the contrary, we only know it to be a law of God because it already commands our inward assent." This is essential Kantism, the gospel of the *Critique of the Practical Reason*, and the *Religion within the Boundaries of mere Reason*. Not ethics, then, from theism, but theism from ethics. Not morality from God, but God is known from and through morality.

Now, here we may be justified in remarking, by way of a preliminary indication of the truth, rather than of an argument, that the preponderant weight of modern philosophical authority is emphatically in favour of some such interpretation of ethic as Cousin sketches from Kant. Whatever the cry of "back to Kant" may actually mean, an idealist ethic is in the air of the schools of this country and America. I am not oblivious of such names as Spencer and Stephen, nor of Höffding or Gizycki abroad, but I think it undeniable that what we mean by the metaphysical implications of ethic commands the assent, not merely of the prophets of the church ethical, such as Emerson, Carlyle and Ruskin, but also of the rising men amongst us who are carrying on the philosophical traditions of the country. But passing by the argument from authority, let us approach the question from the standpoint of reason.

We may appeal, in the first place, to the truth implied in the very expression the *Moral Law*. But it must be explained that by the term moral law we do not mean a code of five, ten, or fifty commandments, but simply the expression of the ethical "ought," the announcement of the supreme fact of moral obligation in general, that is, the duty of unconditionally obeying the right when the right is known to us. It is no more the duty of the moral law to set about codifying laws than it is of the conscience to practise casuistry. Conscience is not a theoretical instructor, but a practical commander. The intelligence, the reason in man it is to which is allotted the function of formulating laws and of deciding what is and what is not in conformity with right. Once that is decided, according to its light, by the reason, then conscience steps in and authoritatively commands that the right is to be unconditionally obeyed. And this, of course, solves that venerable objection that conscience can be no guide because moral codes have changed and are changing, and are not alike in various ages and countries. Conscience has nothing to do with the excesses of Torquemada, or libidinous rites of Astarte. Reason was at fault, not conscience, and that supreme judge, misguided by the reason, appeared to give a false judgment, whereas, true to itself for ever, it simply pronounced in each and every instance, that the right must be obeyed. Like the needle in the compass, it undeviatingly points to the polar star of duty.

Let us proceed with our analysis of the conception of the moral law.

There are various schools of ethics, but they are all united in maintaining *some* obligatory force in morality, that whatever may be the precise meaning of the solemn word right, the right is binding on the allegiance of our will. Hence Emerson, of the rational school, is philosophically accurate when he deduces purity of heart, or uprightness of intention, and the law of gravitation from the same source. They are both laws, one valid in the spheres, the other valid among men, the one only difference being that whereas the spheres compulsorily obey the law of their existence, man by the noble obeisance of his will—an obeisance which, as Kant points out, raises him to an immeasurable dignity—voluntarily submits himself to his law, and thereby fulfils the purpose of his life.

Moreover, we must reflect, as the law of gravitation, which as physical beings we obey, is none of our making, but merely our discovery, so is the moral law, the eternal distinction between right and wrong, no creation of man's. He is born into a world not his own, and he finds himself surrounded by an order which is not within the sphere of his control. The law, for instance, of numbers, the law of thought, the facts of the universe, organic and inorganic, the bases on which he has erected what is compendiously called civilisation—are all provided otherwise than by his efforts. He is born into an order of reason which, by obedience to the law and light of reason within him, he has developed into the stately fabric of organised, social, political, intellectual, in a word, civilised life. But, I would repeat, the basic facts of this life are none of our creation; they are our *discovery*, and no more the *invention* of man than America is the invention of Columbus. Hence, with the master-poet of Hellas, we must acknowledge those—

 agrapta kasphalê theôn
nomima

ou gar ti nun ge kachthes, all aei pote
zê tauta, koudeis oiden ex otou phanê—

the unwritten irresistible laws, ever-living, whose origin no one can tell.

It would be of no avail, I submit, to point out to Sophocles, as Spencer pointed out to Kant, that a knowledge of the early condition of man would have made short work of these sublimities, that the cosmical man was before the ethical man, in whom we discover very little evidence of these majestic laws of such universal and undeniable validity. The reply would be that the growth of them is only evidence of what was potentially present from the first, that just as the beating of brass was no obstacle to the ultimate evolution of the opera or the oratorio, or the first vague feelings of wonderment with which primitive man surveyed himself and his surroundings to the creation of the world of science and philosophy, so the undoubted fact that man was unmoral at the start is no obstacle to the belief that the moral law was as existent then as now. Nay, just as the cosmic process itself from the first contained the promise and potency of an organic form ultimately to be called man and to become "the crowning glory of the universe," so also, we hold, it contained the potentialities of that whereby man was enabled to crown the splendid edifice of creation by the imperishable deeds he has done, and that just as it would be futile to ask one to point out traces of man amongst "the dragons of the prime," or some Bathybiotic slime, so it would be equally irrelevant to demand indications of moral life in the tertiary man. But, as in the savage of to-day, as in the infant, it is there; and the fact that it ultimately appears shows that it was there. So surely as the laws of music, mathematics and thought, are of the Sophoclean category of eternal facts, man's discoveries not his creations, so also are the moral laws, and, therefore, when Mr. Spencer points out the

And, in explaining why pleasure and pain cannot be regarded as "the sovereign masters" of ethic, we may add to the evidence for our conclusion. It appears that Bentham and his school do not observe the proprieties of language in identifying the moral good, the moral right, with pleasure. The ideas are really incommensurate, as is well pointed out in Schurman's monograph on the Kantian and the evolutionary ethics of Spencer. The ethical "ought," the word which gives the keynote to the whole science, does not and cannot mean what is "pleasurable," "serviceable," or "useful". The word essentially implies the "ideal," the conformity to a definite standard of right, the approximation towards a goal or standard of conduct implicitly recognised as absolute good. But the ideas of "pleasurable," "useful," and the like concern the moment only; they merely suggest that man should secure the advantage offered or avoid the pain which may befall him here and now, or some time subsequently to his contemplated action. Hence there is no obligatory force in this ethic. Prudential motives, suggestions of expediency, abundance of counsel, if you will; but we miss the note of authority, the commanding voice, the categorical imperative, the solemn injunction, "Thou canst, therefore thou must". Indeed, it seems difficult to see how one could convince a man on hedonistic or utilitarian grounds that a course of conduct on which he was bent, and to which he was allured by the overmastering impulse of a vehement nature, and which promised him sensible gratification, possibly even material advancement, was not legitimate. I do not press this, nor do I suggest that moral elevation of life is not discernible amongst professors of this interpretation of ethics equally with those who take an idealist view. All I say is, that the recognised terminology of the ethical life, the "ought," the "must," receive an ampler recognition, a fuller interpretation, in the rational schools than in those of Bentham and Spencer.

And, finally, we may approach the question from the point of view of evolution. Everybody knows the pitiless manner in which the late Professor Huxley contrasted the ethical man with the cosmical process, how he pointed out that the one hope of progress lay in man's ability to successfully combat by ethical idealism the rude realism of the material order of which he is a part. The facts need no exposition. Every man has the evidence of it in himself, in the periodical insurrection of the ape and tiger element in him against the authority of some mysterious power which in the course of his long sojourn here has been acquired, and to which he recognises that the allegiance of his life is due. That tearful, regretful expression of the *Grand Monarque*, after one of Massillon's searching, scathing sermons on the sensual and spiritual in every man, "*Ah, voilà deux hommes que je connais très bien!*" may be repeated with even greater truthfulness by every one of us, now that Darwin has superseded St. Paul in the explanation of the phenomenon.

Now, here we have a surprising contradiction in Nature, the startling apparition of an element in man so utterly opposed to all that is beneath him, that a scientific chieftain tells us that his only hope is to kill out that ape and tiger, or at any rate keep it under unceasing control. Whence is this extraordinary human element, and what explanation can be given of the contradiction unless there be some higher synthesis into which the antinomy is taken up and resolved into unity? If out of the primordial nebula both the cosmos and man, with all that he is, have been evolved, then it would appear, plain as the writing on the wall, that some extraordinary transformation has come over the scene as soon as man appeared, and that an element utterly irreconcilable with all that has appeared previously manifests itself in him, not as an accident or a fortuitous occurrence, but as an essential, nay, as *the* essential law of his being.

How can we explain this? How can we account for this complete *volta face* in Nature, which bids man turn his back on all that made the universe and him, and resolve to live by a law so irreconcilable with the methods of the cosmos, that I take it we should be justified in saying that had it been in operation before man Nature itself could not have been evolved?

We believe the contradiction receives its explanation in the synthesis already suggested, that above the two processes, the cosmical and ethical, there is another, that of absolute intelligence or mind, energising through them both from first to last, but in widely different ways. In the cosmos, by ways which we describe as non-moral; in us by law, which we recognise as moral. In every grade of being, in every stratum of Nature, the self-same ever-active Mind is manifest, nay, the very distinctions of Nature's life are fixed by the intenser or remisser energy wherewith the eternal Mind functions in them. From first to last it is mind-power behind all and in all. "In the beginning was Mind; in the beginning was the Reason." Lao-tze is right; the Alexandrian mystic is right; *En archê ho Logos*, and the Mind was the light of man, the light of reason, the holier light of conscience, leading him if he will but follow it, in the way which has been described in language of philosophic precision by the Hebrew poet as "the way everlasting".

Man may sing a *Magnificat*, because mighty things have been done in him, such as a cosmos or an infinity of worlds never knew or shall know. And thus the very contradictions manifested by evolution do but contribute to the truth of the general conclusion, that there is a Power, not dead, dull, inert, but an ever-living, ever-energising Mind, whence the mighty procession set forth, unto which it is ever returning. There is a Power above the water floods and cosmic disasters which is bringing to fulfilment purposes known from everlasting, which we are compelled to acknowledge as beneficent. We see its workings in history, in the rise and fall of nations;

we witness the morally, no less than the physically, unfit fall out of the ranks. Progress here and there may seem to stop, but the course of things is "never wholly retrograde". Is not that hope strong in every man of us, going before us as an unquenchable light, encouraging us to persevere even to the end, because we shall not be deprived of the fruits of our toil, and no demon power shall come to dash the cup of happiness which we have striven to fill?

And what is this but to confess that the Power manifested in the cosmos is identical with the Power manifested in life, that physical and psychical are ultimately one, that virtue and well-being are indissolubly associated? What is this but to confess the supreme synthesis, embracing all apparent contradictions, the ultimate harmony in which all discords are ultimately merged and lost for ever? What is it finally but to proclaim our faith one with that of the most eloquent voice heard in this century, poet and philosopher in one, the sublime Victor Hugo: "*La loi du monde matériel, c'est l'équilibre, la loi du monde moral c'est la justice*"? Pindar's words again! "Justice is rightful sovereign of the world." The Reason which is revealed as equilibrium in the spheres, reveals itself as justice among men. Both spring from one indefectible source. "*Dieu se retrouve à la fin de tout.*"

[1] Lao-tze, quoted in Huc's *China*, vol. ii., p. 177.

IV.

IMMANUEL KANT, THE ETHICAL PHILOSOPHER.

To think of what Immanuel Kant has been to the many men and women of this century, who, having unlearnt the old traditions, had not yet found a new inspiration—the souls that were athirst for the waters of life which the ancient wells could no longer supply—is to be reminded of the pious and generous tribute which the Jewish exiles, after their sad return from the Babylonian captivity, paid to Nehemiah and his brethren, the reorganisers of their race. "Let Nehemiah," they said, "be a long time remembered amongst us, who built up our walls that were cast down, who raised also the bars of the gates!" Precious indeed is the man who can recreate the shattered fabric of the Commonwealth, re-enkindle the pure flame of patriotism, and restore the inspiration of religion. A benefactor indeed is the thinker who can give us a glimpse of the Divine on rational terms, satisfy the exigencies of the intelligence without denying the cravings of the heart, and provide an idealism for the inspiration and guidance of life.

Perhaps it is not too much to say that the temporal destitution of the repatriated Jews was a symbol of the religious and ethical decay of the last century. Protestantism of the orthodox type, which essentially was and is nothing more than the substitution of a book for a Pope, the pruning of the tree dogmatical, the lopping off of some of its more reprehensible excrescences, had visibly failed to meet the necessities of "the irresistible maturing of the human mind," to quote an expression of Emerson's. The older Church had prophesied accurately enough that Lutheranism would turn out but a half-way house to infidelity, and sure enough it did. Its thorough application of the principle of private judgment in matters of religion could no more justify the inspiration of Leviticus than the federal headship of Adam and the dogma of endless vindictive punishment. Hence Lutheranism necessarily meant the gradual disintegration of dogma, that is, of all super-rational truth, for every man "outside the sacred circle of those bound over not to think".

When we remember, in addition to the decay of Protestantism, that Roman Catholic countries afforded more than sufficient evidence of the inability of their own religion to meet the increasing needs of the age—how France, Spain, and Portugal were devastated by the sceptical disease; how they insisted on and carried the total suppression of the Jesuit Order, beyond compare the ablest body of men their Church had ever produced; how the French Revolution was in its inception profoundly anti-Christian, and in its progress even anti-religious—when, I say, we call to mind these facts, we are able to appreciate the accuracy of the statement that, through the maturing of the intelligence of man, the ancient traditions had lost their hold, not only of Protestant, but of Catholic, lands. Without leaving for a moment the eighteenth century, I think we are warranted in stating that the close of the nineteenth century does not witness a rehabilitation of those traditions. The truth is more obvious than ever that in the men of to-day,

> The power is lost to self-deceive
> With shallow forms of make-believe.

Now, it would appear that Immanuel Kant was the man of destiny for the work of the reorganisation of ethical and religious life. I look upon him as the morning star of the New Reformation. He witnessed in his own day the very low-water mark of scepticism, reaching even to the gross atheism of Holbach in the *Système de la Nature.* He had the advantage of everything which David Hume, "the Prince of Agnostics," as Mr. Huxley styled him, found to say, and indeed Hume exercised a marked influence on his German brother-savant, as we may, perhaps, later see. The whole work of the *Encyclopaedia* in France was done under his eyes; the galaxy of brilliant writers who composed that school were contemporaries of Immanuel Kant. He witnessed the crash which accompanied the downfall of the old regime in France, the enthronement of anarchy in the place of government, the complete eclipse of religion, and the worship of reason symbolised on the altar of Nôtre Dame as my tongue refuses to describe. It was the era of the deluge: the water-flood had burst upon Europe; and there was nothing, no institution of State or Church, no philosophy, no religion then extant that could stem the rush of the torrent. Never was the effeteness of ancient systems, the impotence of the old idealism, more conspicuous. In the midst of this wreckage the problem of reconstruction had to be faced. Immanuel Kant did face it, and his object was to provide against the recurrence of atheisms and anarchies, to make godlessness and revolutions impossible, to ensure religion's being a help instead of a gross and deplorable hindrance to progress, and to provide man with an idealism and an enthusiasm which would satisfy his utmost desire for knowledge, and yet stir the pulses of his moral being by the suggestion of an irresistible emotion.

Such I conceive to have been the work which Immanuel Kant undertook in the system of the transcendental philosophy.

The name of this thinker is so famous, I had almost said so venerable, in the ethical Church, that I may be allowed to put before my readers, who may be unacquainted with the details, a few personal or biographical notices concerning him.

Immanuel Kant was born at Königsberg, in Prussia, on 22nd April, 1724, of humble parentage. He was apparently destined for the Church, since his first efforts were directed towards the study of theology in the university of his native town. But natural science and philosophy proved of far more powerful attraction, and, abandoning Divinity, he earned his livelihood, first of all, by acting as a private tutor in the neighbourhood of Königsberg, and afterwards by assuming a similar office in his own university. He subsequently, at the age of forty-six, became a professor of the Philosophical Faculty, a post he retained till his death in 1804. The deep reverence and religious emotion which betrays itself in Kant's ethical writings was probably due to the influence of his parents. His father was venerable in his eyes as a man of moral worth. Honesty, truth and domestic peace characterised his home. For his mother the philosopher cherished the tenderest of recollections, and to her religious feeling, detached as it was completely from formula and system, he probably owes the fervour with which he speaks—as do Emerson and Carlyle—of the sublimity of the moral laws, and of the infinite dignity of a life lived in harmony with them. When he lost his father at the age of twenty-two, he wrote in the family Bible: "On the 24th of March my dearest father was called away by a blessed death. May God, who has not vouchsafed him great pleasure in this life, grant him the joy eternal!"

After a youth spent under the spell of such surroundings, we are not surprised to learn that Kant was of a singularly grave, gentle and quiet demeanour, which in old age tended to deepen into austerity and increased conscientiousness, were that possible, in the fulfilment of his duties. With the simple words, "It is the time," his servant Lampe called him every morning at five minutes to five, and never to the end, according to the testimony of his servant, was the summons disobeyed. In the thirty-four years of his professorship he was reported to have been only once absent from his chair, and that owing to indisposition.

Kant lived a solitary life; he never married. Like more than one eminent man in the past and present, absolute want prevented his inviting the woman he loved to share his lot. The world has just learnt that Tennyson was engaged to his wife for twenty years, from her seventeenth to her thirty-seventh year, owing again to stress of circumstances, and there is living now one eminent man for whom, as for Immanuel Kant, comfort, competence, and fame have come too late to allow of any share in the blessing and joy of home. Such things cannot but deepen the hold these elect spirits have and shall have upon men unto all time.

Of religion Kant conceived a noble idea, but he did not find it realised in the Churches of his day. Sacerdotalism, even in its mildest forms, was abhorrent to him. During his manhood he never entered a church door, a fact which is a source of deep pain to many of his most enthusiastic biographers. Once only did Kant take his place in the procession which made its way to the cathedral on an especial day in the year, and was joined by the rector and professors of the university, but on arriving at the door he turned back and spent the hour of service in the retirement of his rooms. To his free soul it was a performance, professional and sectarian, and in consequence, something of a profanation. His disciple Hegel must have been moved by similar feelings when he replied to the questioning of his old housekeeper why he did not attend Divine service, "Thinking is also a Divine service!"

Nature had an irresistible fascination for him. He learnt that also from his revered mother, whose joy it was to take her child into the world of Nature, where the Soul of the worlds is so conspicuously at work, and instil into his young heart a deep and tender love for the beautiful life around him. Thus he couples the impressive spectacle of the holy night, revealed in the shining of the eternal stars, with the supreme object of emotion, the moral law within the heart, as the most awful of realities.

But not only for Nature in her sublimer aspects did he conceive so reverential a feeling, the humbler exhibitions of beauty and wisdom were equally moving to his awakened spirit. Once he told his friends, whom he constantly had with him at his dinner-table, he had held a swallow in his hands and gazed into its eyes; "and as I gazed," he said, "it was as if I had seen heaven". The great lesson of Mind in Nature he had learnt well at his mother's knee, and he never forgot it. Children, so recently come out from one eternity, their souls so well attuned to the wonderment and mystery there lies hid in things, are peculiarly susceptible to such beautiful influences. Nature is the temple in which their tender souls should learn their first lessons in worship and see the earliest glimpses of the Divine.

Kant lived into his eightieth year, surrounded by the homage of Europe, which made him, in a sense, the keeper of its conscience. His ethical treatises caused him to be consulted from the most distant lands on questions of moral import. It is on record that many of his correspondents paid insufficient postage upon their letters—a fact which meant considerable loss for the philosopher. Indeed, so habitual was the forgetfulness of these ethical sensitives that Kant at length refused to take their letters in. After some thirty years of professorship in his own university his marvellous powers began to fail; his memory served him no longer; his great mind could think no more the thoughts sublime. The keen senses grew dull, and the light of his "glad blue eyes" went out. His bodily frame, which by assiduous care he had maintained as a worthy organ of his mind, sank into weakness. His last years, his last hours even, are described by his well-beloved disciple and friend Wasianski with a faithful and pathetic minuteness which, in the view of some of the great thinker's deepest admirers, might well have been less microscopic. The spectacle of a great mind losing itself at length in the feebleness of age, almost the imbecility of second childhood, might well, they consider, have been withdrawn from the vulgar gaze. "Yet," as the late Prof. Wallace most truly remarks, "for those who remember, amid the decline of the flesh, the noble spirit which inhabited it, it is a sacred privilege to watch the failing life and visit the sick chamber of Immanuel Kant." [1]

On the 12th of February, 1804, in his eightieth year, he passed away, the victim of no special ailment or disease, but exhausted by the life of deep and strenuous thought upon the most profound and sacred problems which can agitate the mind of man. Simple and unostentatious to a degree during his life, the great master left instructions that he was to be buried quietly in the early morning. But for once his wish was disregarded, and amid the mourning of his Alma Mater, his townsfolk and the neighbourhood around, he was laid to rest in the choir of the University Church, which during life he would never enter. As with Kant so with Darwin, all men instinctively feel—even the most narrow of sectarians—that the lives of such men were —I will not say religious—but religion, and so they lay them at last within the shadow of their altars as the worthiest and best of the race. It shows us how deeply seated is the ethical emotion in man; it shows us that the religion of every man at his best moments is such as Immanuel Kant described and realised in his calm and beautiful life—a religion based on the sublime realities of the moral law.

And now, perhaps, we may say something of the thoughts of our philosopher, though at present it cannot be more than of a fragmentary character. If the ethical movement is to prove enduring, the name and teaching of Immanuel Kant must be frequently before us, and numberless opportunities afforded for an ampler account of his doctrine. For the moment my purpose was rather to put before my readers some idea of the man himself whose teaching is now exercising so deep an influence on the religious tendencies of the hour.

Every time you read of the vicar of a parish changing pulpits with his Nonconformist brother; every philanthropic meeting you hear of as addressed by clergymen of all denominations; every garden party given by a bishop or a dean to a Dissenters' Conference; every advance you gratefully note towards a wise and patient tolerance of theological dissensions, the sinking of sectional differences in the interests of a higher and purer life—ascribe it all to the beneficent influence of Immanuel Kant. Before his day all these fraternisings would have been impossible; the ancestors of these reconciled brethren were ready to scourge and burn each other, until Kant came and shamed them out of their narrowness and bigotry. Men talk no more of "mere morality," as though it paled into positive insignificance by the side of the dogmatical majesty of articles and creeds. Kant has taught them "a more excellent way," and in so far as they have learnt that one lesson, they and we are members of the one great Church—the Church of the ethically redeemed, the Church of men to come—the idealism, the enthusiasm, of the ages to be. Never let it be forgotten. We are not concerned to controvert or to destroy. The message of Kant to the Churches is that in all essentials we are at one with them, and the trend of thought is now setting visibly towards the substitution of an ethical for a doctrinal basis of religion. You are powerless to resist the times, we would urge. Whether the old names and formulae survive or not, "the irresistible maturing of the general mind" will make it impossible for men to acquiesce in any religious belief not grounded on the conviction that the sole test of a man's status is not what he believes, but what he does. This is Kant, this is Christ, and this is the message of the ethical Church.

But to return to the teaching of the philosopher of ethics, I must remind my readers again that I am unable to do more than sketch the outlines of the great ethical system which he gave to the world. More than that will not be needed for the moment. But before undertaking even a synoptical account of the transcendental ethic, I think it advisable to remark that Kant's title to philosophical immortality rests upon his constructive work as an ethicist, and not on his critical work as a speculative thinker. It is well known that the two philosophies of Kant are not *primâ facie* harmonious, that he finds himself compelled to deny as a critic that of which he is most certain as a moralist. Thus the great facts of theism, immortality and the autonomy or freedom of the will, he professes himself unable to know save as revelations of the moral order. His mind, or pure reason, can know nothing of them; it is his will or practical reason which discerns them as plain deductions from the overwhelming fact of the moral law. This fact has led some critics to describe Kant as a sceptic. Nothing could be farther from the truth. We might almost quote of him what Browning wrote of Voltaire:—

> Crowned by prose and verse, and wielding
>   with wit's bauble learning's rod,
> He at least believes in soul and is very sure of God.

No one more so; yet as a thinker he professed himself unable to *demonstrate* these high truths. In that sense Kant's famous *Critique of the Pure Reason* may be described as the forerunner of the systematic agnosticism which is set forth in the *First Principles* of Mr. Spencer. But there is this immense difference, that Kant was convinced of the reality of that which the mind of man could not demonstrate. The great facts were existent indeed, but he was powerless to reach them with the instruments at his command. In consequence, he laid it down as a principle that man must ever act as though it were actually demonstrated that we were free, our innermost being imperishable, and a supreme judge and dispenser of justice to administer the moral laws which are the guide of life. It would be out of place to state the arguments whereby Kant justified his belief in a controlling mind in the universe and in the spiritual nature of man, while avowing his inability to demonstrate those truths. It must suffice to state here that the truths which lie at the foundation of religion were a matter of profound conviction with the sage of Königsberg, all the deeper perhaps because he would not claim to subject them to an intellectual dissection or to be able to measure out heaven and earth in the exiguous terms of human thought.

But as soon as he leaves the plane of the pure or speculative reason and rises to the level of the practical reason or the will, then the full truth bursts upon his astonished gaze, clearer than the meridian light. He sees no more "half shade, half shine," but the truth pours itself "upon the new sense it now trusts with all its plenitude of power". It is the will, not the mind, which discloses the full revelation to Immanuel Kant, and makes him the deeply-reverent, religious man he ever was, the convinced theist, the believer in his power to control his acts by the independence of his will, and in the possibility, or rather the certainty, of his being one day morally perfect—not indeed within the limits of the life which now is, but in a future life of unlimited duration. That which to Wordsworth was an intimation was to Kant an intuition after the vision of the glory of the moral law had flooded his innermost soul.

And this we may, perhaps, briefly show before bringing the chapter to an end.

The fundamental principle of the Kantian system is the primacy of the will. The key to the mystery of man's being Kant finds, not in the marvellous faculty of intelligence, but in that power of self-movement, that capacity for self-originated energy which we call the will. Reason is "regulative," he said, but not "creative" and "constitutive," like the will. It is the latter faculty which makes us what we are, determines our life, fixes our character, and decides our destiny. As you act, so you are. This principle once conceded, the majestic system at once takes shape. What is it that governs the world of phenomena outside us? Physical laws, and supreme amongst these laws, that of equilibrium or gravitation. What is it that governs the reason? The laws of thought, those aboriginal rules, none of man's creation, but the essentially necessary guides which he was bound to discover and to follow if he is to think accurately, that is, if his thoughts are to be in conformity with fact. And what is it which governs the will of man? "Do you tell me," the master would urge, "that the inert masses of the spheres have each their own movements regulated for them, that nothing from a stone to a star is shaped or moved without the intervention of eternal laws; that the lispings of children no less than the meditations of a philosopher must conform to law, and that the will of man, whereby he makes himself to be what he is, shapes his character, influences his surroundings, and fixes his destiny—do you venture to say that that is lawless in a world where all is law? No," he proclaims in words which burn conviction into his soul: "it, too, has its laws, the highest, holiest thing in all this universe, the law of laws which confronts man wherever he goes, fills all his sublimest thoughts, subdues his soul to the most reverent worship, and is the holiest inspiration of his religion. It is the moral law, the supreme concern of the will of man, a revelation to man alone of his own unspeakable dignity, the norm or standard whereby he is to regulate his life —this it is which is the law of his will. As gravitation rules the stars, so the moral law, the sanction of the eternal distinction between right and wrong, controls the will, not compulsorily, not arbitrarily, as though it could by any possibility be otherwise, but freely. So sovereign is its power, so authentic are its claims, that if it had might as it has right, it would rule the world." It is, therefore, to use Kant's own language, a *categorical imperative*, that is, an unconditional command. "Thou canst, and therefore thou must." By the very manhood you possess you are bound wholly to surrender yourself in submission to what you know to be the right for the right's sake alone. You must make it your own law, and obey it as inflexibly as the stars keep their courses in the everlasting way.

>   Thou dost preserve the stars from wrong,
> And the most ancient heavens, through thee, are fresh and strong.

We may see now how Kant bases his whole system upon the indestructible fact of ethical law, the primeval intuition of the awakened spirit of man into the eternal distinction between good and evil. Standing on that foundation, he is able to descry the world of transcendental realities—"the land which is very far off"—which the pure and critical reason could never behold. But though the eyes of the mind were holden, the intuition of the will enables him to gaze direct into the unseen and discern freedom, soul, immortality and God as eternal facts. For whence this sublime law of life unless we conceive mind, not blind chance, as the arbiter of things? Whence this constraining power within me, exerting itself to the uttermost to win my allegiance to the right, unless I am free to obey or disobey? How is not the very conception of morality entirely obliterated in the false philosophy that would fain persuade man that because he is *in* the world he must needs be *of* it, and because the tides rise and fall with the phases of the moon, that his actions are fixed and controlled by influences utterly beyond his power? We have no room for the "man-machine" in the beautiful school of Immanuel Kant.

And, finally, the awful question of the future Kant solves in the light of the same sublime principle. "That law," he urges, "which is the essential law binding humanity must one day be fulfilled in every one of us. There is a moral as well as a physical evolution which you try in vain to confine to the limits of the life which now is. There is no argument known to science justifying such an attempt." Kant believes in the Eternities, because every man born of woman is destined to be at last in absolute conformity with that law of everlasting righteousness which is for us what the law of balance is to the infinite worlds. All life, that which now is and whatever is to be in the hereafter, is simply a never-ending progress towards an ideal whose dignity is infinite. Hence the command of Jesus, "Be ye perfect as your heavenly Father is also perfect," would be endorsed by Kant as in strict harmony with the philosophy which does not teach that the physical act of dissolution called death fixes the moral state of man for ever, but that all life, whatsoever it may be and wheresoever it may be lived, is but an approach towards a goal of infinite value, the will of man absolutely conformed to justice, or the moral law.

As Kepler described the philosopher and the scientist as "thinking again the thoughts of God," even so does the Kantian ethic aspire to absolute conformity of will with that Will which is supreme and eternal, the moral order itself personified. This is immortality: this is everlasting life, even as the Christian disciple and philosopher describes it: "This world passeth away and the desire thereof, but he that doeth the Divine will endureth for ever". The phenomenal world is a pageant, a scene. Only "the good will" (Kant's constant expression) in absolute harmony with the Supreme Will is real and eternal.

[1] *Philosophical Classics*, p. 85.

V.

THE ETHICAL DOCTRINE OF COMPENSATION.

I suppose there is no teaching more frequently insisted upon in the Old and in the New Testament as the truth of a judgment, now, or in the future, upon the misdeeds or sins of men. Let criticism prune and cut as it will, while it exhibits the deplorably low standard of morality once prevalent among the Hebrew peoples, and therefore prevalent among their Gods, their Elohim, Adonai and Jahveh, one thing, at least, is undeniable—that that which is recognised as immoral is reprobated and forthwith visited with condign punishment. Doubtless, acts which to us are wholly reprehensible are discussed without attaching any stigma to them, and are even permitted, and sometimes suggested, by Jahveh himself, as in the story of Judith and Holofernes. Such ethical insensibility is wholly natural, viewing the state of development at which the Hebrew people had arrived, and should cause no wonderment in those who are familiar with the Deity of Christian Mediaevalism, and the methods and practices he was supposed to favour. But what should be carefully noted is, that nothing is adjudged immoral but is forthwith sternly reprobated and condemned to a fitting retribution. "The way of transgressors is hard" was a conviction with the race. In the same way, the ethical note rings out in the New Testament, that right and wrong are eternally dissevered, sheep ever separated from goats; that virtue must be rewarded and vice be condemned and punished.

Now, this teaching of the judgment to come, the bare announcement of which by Paul filled Felix, the Roman governor, with such dire consternation, is the subject of which we propose to set forth the philosophical and ethical explanation. In the Bible we have the mythical setting much as we have the mythical version of the agony of spirit undergone by Christ before he definitely committed himself to his prophetical work. It is for us to-day to disentangle the substantive truth from the maze of legend with which an imperfectly developed age has surrounded it and discover the true *raison d'être* of that doctrine which "the Bible Christian" confesses under the aspect of the "Last Judgment".

Now, I take it that no educated man believes in the drama, or rather, the panorama, of the "last judgment"; the vision of Jesus sitting in the clouds, with every human being that ever was or shall be gathered before his throne to hear definite sentence pronounced upon them. The *mise-en-scène* demands of course the presence of bodies, and I suppose it is needless to point out the dogma of the resurrection of the body, insisted upon by all the Christian Churches, is a blank impossibility. We may acquire other bodies in that unknown state, should we stand in need of such appurtenances—a fact which we may wholly disbelieve—but of one thing we may rest assured, that these identical bodies in which we die can by no possibility conceivable to us be brought back.

I once read a highly imaginative article in a religious magazine which attempted to solve the unsolvable by suggesting that after men's bodies had been buried in sufficient numbers, the whole soil of our planet would consist of nothing but the substance of the bodies of the dead, and that when that momentous epoch arrived, the Almighty would give the order for the sounding of the final trump, and the whole solid globe would be forthwith transmuted, or rather re-transmuted, into human bodies—in what condition it was not stated—for the countless myriads of "souls" ready to take possession of them. Probably, this pious romance was woven in the days before cremation, and as the next century will not be very old before we shall be compelled to resort to that method of disposal of the dead, at all events in our larger cities, it becomes increasingly difficult to comprehend how men of the future, to say nothing of the past, are going to be provided with their own bodies so as to put in an appearance at the great assize.

We may rightly wonder how men and women of the nineteenth century can still believe in the Churches and Chapels which teach such deplorable absurdities as the revelation of God, and how it happens that when religion appears upon the scene of their daily life, their common sense can so totally desert them. One need say nothing of the inadequacy of the judgment pronounced, the summary classification of the myriads of humanity as white sheep or black goats, or the character of the rewards and punishments allotted. The one redeeming point in the narrative is that whatever judgment is pronounced is decided, not on doctrinal grounds, about which no two of Christ's followers can be got to agree, but on ethical grounds, on character manifesting itself in public spirit and care for the unfortunate—the bruised reeds and smoking flax—of our communities. It would seem impossible to maintain after this final scene that creeds and faiths have any decisive influence on our status here or hereafter.

But though now seen to be no more than a variant upon the apocalyptic tradition and literature which represented that Jesus was to return speedily to earth and rule among his saints for a thousand years—a delusion which apparently possessed even the trained intellect of Paul, and subsequently led to the pseudo-Peter explaining that his fellow-Christians must not be in too great a hurry, because "a thousand years are as one day and one day as a thousand years in the sight of the Lord"—it has done an incalculable amount of harm in the past. It has shut men's eyes to the awful fact of retribution, administered here and now, and prevented their realising any punishment other than the savage, barbarous and wholly vindictive punishment of torturing eternally by fire. It shuts men's minds to the operation of moral laws, to the fact that judgment is executed instantaneously upon the commission of wrong. It has, and it does, to the serious detriment of moral development, lead man to put off until late in life, sometimes to the very hour of death itself, restorative work which should have been undertaken immediately on the recognition or conviction of misdeeds. The notion that he is not to be called up for judgment until he is rendered incapable by death of doing any further mischief, has been a moral obstacle in the path of man, and therefore of the race, wholly beyond the power of calculation. Foolish priests once thought that by the invention of the dogma of hell they could terrorise men into morality, and so they preached their Divinity, the magnified copy of a fiend, who would have cheerfully created humanity out of nothing and damned them everlastingly, had not he himself, in the shape of his son, who is one in being with him, decided to appear upon earth and atone to himself for the mischief, which presumably he could have very well foreseen, perpetrated by man.

And what has been the effect of such teaching on humanity? It is impossible to doubt that it has led to results deplorably, indescribably wicked. Whence, for instance, arose the horrors of the mediaeval inquisition, the insensate tortures inflicted upon men like Huss and Bruno solely for theological errors, if not from belief in this demon-deity whom the Church worshipped? If their practices were but a shadow of the horrors he was supposed to be everlastingly inflicting on mankind, who could raise a protest against them? Shall man be juster than his God? This perverse Christian morality is responsible for the worst cruelties which have tormented the human race since the days of ecclesiastical domination. If the Deity is inhuman, why should man be otherwise? Therefore, inhuman tortures will be inflicted on prisoners. The rack and thumb-screw will be used to extract secrets. Men will be immured alive within narrow walls and allowed to perish by inches. The Austrian prisons in the northern Italian provinces will be so constructed that the miserable victim can neither sit nor lie down nor see the light of day. Floggings and scourgings will be universal, *lettres de cachet* an institution. Why not? Where the god has no sense of justice, why should man? Hundreds and hundreds of thousands of victims will perish at the stake and in the flames in atrocious agony because they are wizards or witches or have had dealings with imaginary devils. Why not? The god does worse than all this. He keeps his victims alive for the sole purpose of glutting his ire and satiating his insatiable vengeance. Nay, things are so ordered that the very happiness of the elect is enhanced, not only by the knowledge, but by the sight, of the appalling, unavailing anguish of the lost, and we have seen such a philosopher as Aquinas representing the Deity as conducting the "elect" in troops and droves to the heavenly shores and giving them "a glimpse of hell" by way of stimulating their enjoyment of the celestial beatitude. Why not? I ask again. My only wonderment is how we ever got rid of it. Picture the world under the universal dominion of this foul superstition. It reigns on the thrones of kings, in the cabinets of statesmen, it is preached in the pulpits, taught in the schools, it is the earliest lesson that trembles on the lips of innocent children. The most ingenious, subtly contrived, widespread and all-pervading influence is especially created to propagate it everywhere in the shape of the Christian Church—a Divine institution, possessed of the keys of life and death, of heaven and hell—the sole representative of the Deity on earth. How, we ask, in wondering gratitude, did the world ever escape the tyranny of such superstition? This fact alone—this deliverance—is enough to make one believe that there is a "Power, not ourselves, which makes for righteousness," that the course of human events is never wholly retrograde.

And, now, what is the truth about the "judgment to come"? What is the ethical equivalent of "hell fire"? In the first place, we refuse to believe in a "last judgment" because we know that judgment is not only pronounced but executed instantaneously, automatically, I would say, on the commission of wrong. There is no need to wait for the day of judgment or even for the hour of death. If a man has done wrong he sits condemned that self-same moment. *Illo nocens se damnat quo peccat die*. There is no need of God, angel or devil, to announce the fact or deliver judgment; the man has pronounced his own sentence, executed judgment on himself. This is, in essence, the ethical doctrine of compensation, that this universe is so woven, that the nature of things is such that "things are what they are, that the consequences of things will be what they will be," that we can no more hope to avert them by crying out for help to man, saint or God, than we can hope to hurl back the waves that dash upon the strand at flood tide. Our view is that moral laws are as irresistible as physical, and admit of no more dispensation than the everlasting order of Nature. One of our main reasons for repudiating the conception of the miraculous is that it involves a violation of eternal order and therefore of eternal reason, and if freely admitted in the physical, would doubtless be speedily introduced into the moral order, to the destruction of civilised society. We believe that this universe is "so magically woven" that it is absolutely impossible to escape the consequences of our deeds, and if the Buddhist doctrine of Karma represents that teaching, then we are among its most enthusiastic adherents, because it is absolutely true to fact.

But let us look at the matter more closely.[1]

Have we ever sufficiently reflected how that "all things are double, one against the other," in this mysteriously governed world, that everything has its counterpart? the world appears to be split into halves, which yet cleave to each other, as a man is haunted by his shadow. "An inevitable dualism bisects Nature, so that each thing is half, and suggests another thing to make it whole." Thus—spirit, matter; man, woman; odd, even; subjective, objective; in, out; upper, under; action, rest; yea, nay. "All things are double, one against the other."

All the woes of existence arise from our deliberate resistance to the law of oneness, to that integration which is so conspicuous in Nature. We are incessantly seeking to take the one half and leave the other, and straightway Nemesis overtakes us. We want to enjoy the pleasures of sense without attending to the inexorable requirements of mind, and such an appalling satiety sickens our souls, that we forget ourselves in the commission of deeds unspeakably wicked; we possibly degrade ourselves in the eyes of all men by falling even into the clutches of the law, or we border on the verge of self-destruction in our unspeakable *ennui*. We would have the half, while Nature planned the whole, and we pay the last farthing. The results are naturally so appalling that it is not to be wondered that men sought to express them under the image of a fire which will not be quenched, a worm of remorse which can never die—an immense despair for which there is no relief.

Life is full of distressing illustrations of this ethical law. A man who owns but the clothes he wears one day, is a millionaire the next, and he attempts the impossible task of bisecting life, which has been manifestly planned as a whole. He appears to succeed for a time, but one day men are startled to hear that he has owned up that he had chosen the wrong path, and has determined to quit it in suicide. A few months after, the community is compelled to witness an almost unparalleled degradation, that of a young man born in the purple, with every advantage that birth, position, education or matrimonial connections could give him, sentenced as a felon for the meanest treachery, because he would halve life which was planned a whole, and forgot the Fates, the dread Erynys, who administer the ethical law of compensation.

But it is the same in lesser as in greater things. Without hesitation, we may ascribe our minor sorrows to the one self-same source, the attempt to dissever the sensual sweet, the sensual strong, the sensual bright, from the moral sweet, the moral deep, the moral fair. We forget that purity of heart and the law of gravitation arise in the same eternal spring, that the world is a whole, that moral and physical are grounded in one source, and we pay the penalty. "The soul says eat; the body would feast. The soul says the man and woman shall be one flesh and one soul; the body would join the flesh only. The soul says, Have dominion over all things to the ends of virtue; the body would have power over things to its own individual ends."

Now, this conduct never yet met with any success. You thrust your arm into the stream to divide the water, but it re-unites behind your hand. You attempt to live your life on one side only, to dissever that which was made for unity, and calamity comes to crush you. Men and women marry for flesh or gold, they put half their whole into the contract, and their sacrilegious bargain smites them with a curse. It is the law of compensation, the workings of that moral gravitation which causes all things to fit into their own places, and is to us the clearest indication of the workings of the Divine in all this tumultuous life.

Wonderful discernment of the ethical prophet! We cease to see God omnipresent in all things, and our blindness ends in our destruction. We see the sensual allurement, but not the sensual hurt; we see the mermaid's head, but not the dragon's tail; we think we see our way to cut off that which we would have from that which we would not have. "How secret art Thou who dwellest in the highest heavens in silence, that bringest penal blindnesses on such as have unbridled desires," quotes Emerson from Augustine's confessions.

No "last judgment," then, but a first judgment, a judgment here and now, swift, sudden, irreversible upon every man and woman who dare to take their lives by halves, to forget the seamless unity wherewith the universe is woven. This is the ancient doctrine of Nemesis, who keeps watch in the universe and lets no offence go unchastised. The Furies are the attendants on justice, and if the sun in the heavens should transgress his path, they would punish him.

This is that awful yet sublime doctrine of retribution which is the groundwork of the masterpieces of the ancient Greek tragedies, the inspiration without which the world would never have known the Agamemnon or the immortal trilogy of Sophocles. It is the doctrine which made Plato describe punishment as going about with sin, "their heads tied together," and Hegel define it as "the other half of sin," while Emerson shows that "crime and punishment grow out of one stem. Punishment is a fruit which, unsuspected, ripens with the flower of pleasure which concealed it." They are linked together inexorably, as cause and effect, and no god can dispense in this law, because the law itself is God.

Hence, there can be no such thing as "forgiveness of sin". An act once done is irreparable. Its consequences must endure to all time. Our most agonising repentance cannot undo the past, it can only avail to safeguard the future. We cannot escape the law of compensation. There is no magnified man in the skies, swayed by human passions, ready, at the call and entreaty of prayer, to obstruct the operation of natural laws. Theories of atonement by blood shedding, sacrifices for the forgiveness of sins, arose in the days when man believed in such a deity as that, but we know none such now, and wise are we if we recognise—oh, how well it had been if in our youth we all could have known—that the consequences of an act are absolutely inevitable, that deeds once done, words once spoken, are traced ineffaceably on the tablets of universal nature and must reverberate throughout the universe to all time!

Severe teaching, you say. Yes, one pauses here when thoughts of hell and devils never once made man pause. The truth is, no one really believes the insensate teaching of the Churches on punishment. Even their adherents have outgrown them. Nothing is clearer from history than that fear of hell fire never yet made man moral. It could not keep the Church of mediaevalism, its priests and its bishops, aye, and its supreme pontiffs—numbers of them—even decent living men, to say nothing of morality or virtue. It is worse than useless now;—an insult to reason and an outrage on religion. But what *will* hold a man is the doctrine of compensation, of judgment pronounced *by himself* directly his iniquity is accomplished, of sentence self-executed, unpardonable and irremissible, now and for ever.

And, added to this, the conviction that his crimes are committed, not "against God," who can in no wise be personally influenced or injured by man's misdeeds, being wholly destitute of human passions and emotions, but against his fellow man, or against his sister woman.

One knows, alas! the beginning of the end to which the lost have come. If only youth had been taught in the opening days of life, when impressions are so vivid, that there is no such article as the creeds of the Churches falsely proclaim—"the forgiveness of sin"—that one only wrong act may, rather must, be the starting point which will one day precipitate a catastrophe, how many would have been saved from the nameless depths, of which we must be silent, how many spared the anguish of an unavailing remorse!

Must this false teaching indeed go on for ever? Will it never dawn upon our priests and ministers, our masters and mistresses in schools, that God bears none of the burden of humanity; his heart never breaks because a life is withering in despair? He takes no hurt from the weltering sorrows by which so many are overwhelmed. It is man, it is woman, who bears the agony; the crushing burden of wrong-doing falls on them. Look no more then, we urge, to a phantom deity, to an idol-god in the skies, a figment of a disordered imagination, but think on your brother man before you dare to set mischief in motion. When you apprehend the nearness of danger, think of the future, think of consequences, think only of the irremissibleness of sin, which not all the waters and baptisms, though it were of blood, through which the Churches can pass you, will ever be able to efface.

How much knavery in actual progress in this wilderness of men in London might one not hope to stop if this doctrine of compensation could be brought home? How much company-promoting, fraud, mendacity, adulteration of food, could we not render impossible, if ethical and prophetical teaching took the place of the Church catechisms and the creeds, if men could be persuaded that the success of their ventures—quite legitimate in the eyes of the civil and criminal law—can only be purchased by the tears and ruin of human beings? The dogma of endless future punishment was apparently impotent to restrain the ultra-orthodox directors of the Liberator Company, but I take it that no man who had been schooled in Emerson, could have sat at that board and thanked an Almighty God for the exceptional favours he had been mercifully pleased to bestow on their conscious frauds. The vindictiveness of a purposeless hell has, of course, failed ignominiously as a deterrent from crime. We cannot conceive infinite Intelligence inflicting an excruciating and endless punishment simply for punishment's sake. We are superior to such methods ourselves; we refuse to associate them with God. What we do believe in, what we are sure of, is that a man's sin must find him out, that he must reap as he sows, that the consequences of his misdeeds are eternal, that—

All on earth he has made his own
Floating in air or pent in stone,
Will rive the hills, the sea will swim,
And like his shadow follow him.

[1] In what follows I have freely borrowed from the great "Essay on Compensation".

VI.

CONSCIENCE THE VOICE OF GOD AND THE VOICE OF MAN.

We have already learnt in the study of the doctrine of Compensation that the misfortunes of life are due to man's attempt to bisect the world and life, and seize greedily on one half to the partial or total neglect of the other. Life having been planned a whole, inevitable disaster overtakes the man who would behave as though it were a thing of shreds and fragments. Now this law of what we may call the Divine unity is equally valid in the purely intellectual order. That, likewise, refuses to admit schisms and divisions to break in on the solidity of its unbroken ranks. An attempt to view life and its problems exclusively from our own standpoint, is to fail to grasp truth; our shadow gets projected over the surface, and the light is partially concealed, if not wholly confused. No better illustration of this fact, I believe, could be afforded than that supplied by conscience, the practical dictate of reason which controls the moral life of man.

In days of old when man was nothing in his own or anybody else's eyes, in the ages when he thought to magnify the Deity by belittling himself, an interfering agency of the Divine was necessarily invoked on almost every conceivable occasion; "the hand of God" was seen in every occurrence. From the comparatively minor matters of bodily ailments up to the colossal disasters which nature is capable of inflicting—in all the visible interference of the supra-mundane power was discerned. Those were naturally the days of the "Divine right of kings," when all civil power was held to have been centred in one individual by the express act of the Divinity; those were likewise the days when the conscience of man was exclusively interpreted as the articulate utterance of God. But, inasmuch as man was too ignorant and wicked to rightly interpret that supreme oracle, he was bidden to leave it in the custody of a sanctified corporation, the Church, and to keep his thoughts and his conduct in tune with the dominant ecclesiastical sentiment of the hour.

Now, from that extraordinary position a reaction was of course inevitable. Man could not go on for ever describing himself as "a worm" and an outcast, or avowing himself "a miserable sinner" and a limb of Satan; and consequently, with an awakened sense of human dignity, inspiring him, not with vainglory, but with an ever-deepening self-reverence, the ascription of all agency to supernatural power began to be seriously curtailed. "The Divine right of kings" went its way with other archaisms into the limbo of oblivion, from which the reigning monarch in Prussia would appear to be vainly endeavouring to rescue it, while man began to realise that the causes of natural and human phenomena were to be sought in nature and in man. As a consequence of this, a new theory of conscience began to take shape, which was ultimately described by one of the boldest of later English philosophical writers, the late Professor Clifford, as "the voice of man commanding us to live for the right".[1]

In these definitions of conscience, as "the voice of God" and "the voice of man," we have an instance of propositions which in logic are called *contraries*. Both, therefore, cannot be exclusively and simultaneously true, but both may be simultaneously false. Thus, "all men are white" and "no men are white" are contraries, but they are both false. And this, I submit, is the judgment to be pronounced on these two exclusive definitions of conscience. Neither is, exclusively speaking, true, but there is a measure of truth common to both, and that measure it will be the purpose of the following remarks to determine.

But, before going any farther, we must get a clear idea of what we mean by conscience. In a general way, of course, we all know what is meant by the word: an appeal to conscience would be intelligible by every one. We understand it to be a faculty which decides on a definite course of action when alternatives of good and evil are before us. We look upon it as an instinct, magnetic in its power, incessantly prompting us towards the fulfilment of duty, and gravely reproaching us on its dereliction. We recognise it as the sweetest and most troublesome of visitants; sweetest when the peace unspeakable sinks into our souls, most troublesome when we have been guilty of a great betrayal. So delicate is that voice that nothing is easier than to stifle it; so clear is it that no one by any possibility can mistake it.

Thus, in general terms, we may describe conscience. Coming now more closely to a philosophical analysis of the conception, we shall find therein much enlightenment for the purposes of our present investigation. In the first place, the word is of comparatively late origin. It does not occur in the Hebrew writers of the Old Testament. Its earliest appearance is in the Book of Wisdom, the work of a Hellenistic Jew extremely well acquainted with the trend of Greek thought in the third century B.C. It does not occur in the Gospels, except in the story of the sinful woman whom Christ refused to condemn—a history which, though profoundly in accord with the sympathetic genius of Jesus, is none the less an interpolation in the eighth chapter of the Johannine Gospel, so much so that Tischendorff excised it from his last edition of the text of the New Testament. St. Paul certainly uses the word once in the Epistle to the Romans, and though known in the latter days before the advent of Christianity, we may assume that mainly through that religion the word was popularised throughout the world.

But what is the faculty which corresponds to the word conscience? We shall find etymology of great assistance in giving precision to our thoughts. The word is, of course, a derivative from the Latin, *conscientia*, knowledge with, or together. Now, *scientia* is the simple knowledge of things by the reason, while *conscientia* is the knowledge which the reason has of itself; it is the realisation of one's selfhood—the realisation of the *ichkeit des ego*, as the very expressive German phrase has it, "the selfhood of the I". In English philosophical language we commonly denominate this self-realisation consciousness, a word of precisely the same etymological origin as conscience. If, in the next place, the reason is occupied, not with the reflex action of self-contemplation, but with moral action or the discernment of right from wrong, then it is called, and is, no longer consciousness, but *conscience*. Putting it technically, consciousness is a psychological expression, while conscience is ethical.

Nevertheless, it must be most carefully remembered that the two functions are performed by one and the same reason—immaterial and indivisible in us. Truly speaking, there is no real, but only a conceptual, distinction between the reason of a Darwin elaborating his famous law, realising his selfhood, and acknowledging his obligations to the eminent man—only less so than himself—who had simultaneously lighted on the great discovery of the age—the law of organic evolution. As Paul says of those manifold endowments of the earliest Christians, "A diversity of gifts and a diversity of graces, but in them all worketh the self-same spirit," so say we of the reason at the very heart of our being, the sole, self-sufficing explanation of the multitudinous phenomena of our mental life. Hence we arrive at a definition of conscience as "the practical dictate of the reason in us prescribing obedience to the good and avoidance of the evil". Two elements, therefore, are discernible in this definition: first, reason, as such, pointing out what is good and evil; and, secondly, reason, as conscience, ordaining that the good is to be done and the evil left undone—a distinction to be carefully borne in mind when the problem of conflicting consciences has to be faced; how it comes, for instance, that morality appears to differ in different countries, and even in the same individual at different periods of his life.

But of that nothing further need be said now, but we may immediately pass on to see in what sense conscience, thus explained, is, in the first place, to be accounted the voice of God.

Outside a philosophy avowedly atheist it seems difficult to understand how there can be any doubt that the eternal distinction between right and wrong betokens the presence in this world of men of a supreme power and a supreme mind. "How comes it," let us ask with Emerson, "that the universe is so constituted," that that which we instinctively recognise as good makes for the individual and the general welfare, and that which we must perforce reprobate as evil works uniformly disaster? We recognise that things are unalterably so ordered that by no possibility could lying, slander, malice and hatred be other than intrinsically evil, and their opposites be other than essentially good. But how is it that things are so ordered? Whence these uniformities of approbation and disapprobation? Is there any answer conceivable but that the power responsible for the world is a moral power? Whence is existence itself but from the subsistent source of all being? Whence is life but from one ever-lasting source? Whence is intelligence but from the world's Soul, which is the soul of men? And towering above being, above life and reason, is conscience, the supreme guide, the light enlightening every man that cometh into this world.

    Luce intellettual, piena d'amore,
     Amor di vero ben pien di letizia,
    Letizia die trascende ogni dolzore.

What is this "light intellectual," this "love of the true," so unutterably blissful as to quiet all pain and sorrow, but the radiance of the eternal falling athwart the shadows of this lower life? What is this miraculous monitor—this "man within the breast," as the Stoics called it—but the very articulate utterance of the supreme Reason bidding man to live for the right? No great son of earth ever interpreted it otherwise. From the days when Socrates scattered "the sophist clan" in Athens, and forced men by the irresistible majesty of his own moral elevation to believe in a morality which was more than a string of rules sanctioned by convention; from the hour when he refused to escape from prison because his conscience bade him submit to die;—from the days of the sublime martyrdom of Socrates and Jesus, the noble school of the Stoics, down to the philosophic Titans of the eighteenth and nineteenth centuries in Germany, with the glorious sage of Königsberg at their head, there has been but one answer to the question, What is conscience? Conscience, they proclaimed, is the voice of God. So surely as the maternal instinct in woman is the voice of universal Nature, so surely is conscience the witness in us that we are indeed "sons of God". If that teaching of the "Over-soul" be the truth, then since the Divine is incarnate in every man, by what other voice *can* we be guided than by the Divine utterance commanding us to live by a moral law? We are Divine by nature, by what other law of life should we live?

Or, how are we to explain the appearance of so strange a visitant in a universe which is dominated by the "struggle for existence"? The intellectual difficulty of atheism is so insuperable that we hear of it no more from men of science. I think Mr. Spencer's speculations have given it the *coup de grace*. But difficult as is the question of the origin of the cosmos, far more so is that of conscience. On what principles are we to explain how a world, evolving itself mechanically, cycle after cycle, has eventually produced an element so utterly at variance with itself, an element which puts right before might, self-surrender before the struggle for existence, and the law of pity in place of the survival of the fittest? Is conscience a development of the cosmic process? And, if so, how is such a *volta face* in nature explicable on purely mechanical grounds, even if the process itself were so explicable? And how striking a fact that the last words Mr. Huxley[2] spoke in public should have been devoted to prove that so opposed were the cosmic and ethical processes—in other words, so completely at variance are the law of conscience and the law of evolution—that only by the triumph of the former over the latter is progress possible in the world. Again, I ask, since conscience is not the voice of Nature, of what is conscience the voice and witness if not of one of whom it is written, "In the beginning was Reason; in the beginning was Mind"?[3]

But there is another aspect of the question, and we must now pass on to inquire how far conscience is also "the voice of man commanding us to live for the right". Quite at the beginning of this ethical movement we protested, as plainly as words would allow, our entire allegiance to the teachings of physical science, and our readiness to abandon any doctrine of ethical religion which is disproved by experimental research. So convinced are we of the absolute unity of truth, because with Plato we believe in the unity of its source in the Divine intelligence, that to us it is inconceivable that there should be any fundamental contradiction in the orders of the real and the ideal. Things seen and unseen, the passing and the eternal, both ultimately take their origin in the same source, the Infinite. No finite thing can be the ultimate explanation of the universe, because it itself requires explanation. Hence, whatever science has to tell us about conscience will be enthusiastically acclaimed by us as true equally with what we learn from the masters of the higher experience, the philosophers who break unto us the bread of life.

Now what has experimental science to say about the conscience? It does *not* say that it is the voice of God—a fact by no means calculated to disturb those who remember that physical investigation is not concerned with such speculations. Half the mischief and misunderstandings which occur over these border questions, which are, so to speak, under two jurisdictions, arise from our forgetting in what capacity and by what principles certain well-known scientific men have made pronouncements on matters such as conscience, morality and religion. There are two sides to them, the physical and the hyper-physical or metaphysical. And here it may not be amiss to offer a suggestion that one should mistrust that parrot cry so often heard from men who speak most confidently about that which they know least, that metaphysic is synonymous with unreality, or in plainer words, moonshine. A very little reflection will be sufficient to satisfy us that without the aid of conceptions higher than those of sense-experience—and that is all the word metaphysic means—it would be absolutely impossible to formulate a single scientific generalisation. What is the very concept of law, or system, but a metaphysical idea? To cease to be metaphysical would be to cease to be rational, to have no higher or wider conceptions than those of a dog. Hence, like M. Jourdain, who had been talking prose all his life without knowing it, some of our most daring anti-metaphysicians have been philosophising by the very method they had in their ignorance so contemptuously denounced.

Therefore, when we hear from Mr. Spencer that conscience, so far from being the voice of God, is but "the capitalised instinct of the tribe," an empirical fact established by heredity, just like fan-tails in pigeons; when Mr. Clifford popularises this teaching in St. George's Hall by announcing that conscience is the voice "of man bidding us to live for man," and Mr. Leslie Stephen tells us that the Socratic conception of conscience "is part of an obsolete form of speculation," we know precisely what judgment to pass upon their assertions. They are speaking, one and all, of the historical growth or natural evolution of that rational faculty in man which they, equally with their opponents, describe as the conscience. And keeping within those limits they are strictly accurate in what they say. Who is there that does not know that time was when the inhabitants of Europe were as destitute of moral instincts, and therefore of a conscience, as the Tonga islanders? Who does not know that man, instead of beginning at the top and tumbling headlong to the bottom, really began at the bottom and learnt everything by a very severe discipline in the hardest of all schools, that of experience? Certainly, we are ignorant of none of those things, and therefore readily assent to Mr. Spencer's teaching that conscience is not a fixed criterion of morality, but a faculty in a ceaseless state of transformation, "in a perpetual state of becoming," that its dicta are, in a certain sense, constantly changing and improving with the progress and development of the race. Certainly, as scientists and anthropologists, we should say precisely the same thing. We should recognise the developed conscience in man as obedient to the law of growth equally with his physical organisation, because we know of men now existent in whom the faculty is still in a very rudimentary state. Every advance in humanitarianism, in our treatment of men and animals, is evidence to us of the illimitable capacities of moral expansion in our nature, and therefore of the growth of conscience, or the moral sentiment.

But are we to conclude therefrom that conscience is nothing more than a product of organic evolution? It is a shallow philosophy, a surface system, indeed, which is content with such an estimate, and is only possible in a school of bald empiricism which imprisons man within the boundaries of his sense-experience, and resolves him into a string of feelings bound together, like a rope of sand, by nothing. The truth is, that Mr. Spencer, Mr. Bain, Mr. Mill and the whole *corps* of experimental philosophers are confusing the reality with its outward manifestation or history. Indeed, by their principles they are constrained to do so. Once affirm that nothing

We learn, thus, from the teaching of both schools that conscience is at once the voice of man, the accumulated and concentrated moral experience of the race, but still more the voice of the eternal Reason which is revealed to our wondering eyes in the true, the good and the beautiful. If "this universe in its meanest province is in very deed the star-domed city of God"; if "the glory of the One breaks through it all in every place," what are we to say of that which is higher than the stars, more radiant than the sun, diviner than all worlds—the conscience of man nobly conformed to the great obedience of the everlasting laws? What are we to say of lives such as those of Gotama, Socrates and Christ? Nothing. Like the psalmist of Israel, I am struck dumb in the presence of a vision so majestical. *Deveni in altitudinem maris et silui*: "I came unto the great deeps and I held my peace".

[1] See his well-known essays, "The Ethics of Belief" and "The Ethics of Religion".

[2] Prof. J. Seth, in his *Study of Ethical Principles*, concludes from Mr. Huxley's Romanes lecture that "agnosticism could scarcely have been the final resting place for such a mind".

[3] I have ventured to repeat here a portion of the argument set forth in the chapter on "Ethics and Theism".

VII.

PRIESTS AND PROPHETS.

One of the most striking characteristics of the ecclesiastic, as opposed to the religious mind, is its tendency to concentrate its attention upon detail to the exclusion of fundamental principles. We are assured that the same habit distinguishes the statesman from the party man, or mere politician. At any rate, we have had abundant evidence during the past fifty years—evidence which has been emphasised during the past year—that the love of detail, of all that comes under that washing of cups and platters, of first places and salutations in the market-place, resplendent raiment and broad phylacteries, which Jesus so summarily denounced in the official religion of his own time, is still a mark of the ecclesiastic temper in the England of to-day. If a man—even though that man be a pope—should question the validity of its "orders," volleys of sacerdotal refutation are fired from the press, the whole atmosphere is electric with the controversial charges such profanity provokes. But let a man proclaim that there is no such institution as "orders" at all, that true religion, that Christianity, as conceived by its founder, is destitute of ritual, priest and sacrifice, and everything is still as a Quakers' meeting. How is it that men will seriously devote their energies to repelling such side attacks as those directed against them by rival churches, while they totally neglect to satisfy an enlightened age as to the validity of the fundamental assumption on which their entire system reposes? The pope and the Eastern Churches may be serious rivals in the camp ecclesiastic, but what are our native pontiffs and priests to reply to men like Hatch, Jowett and Stanley, to say nothing of Martineau, who roundly proclaim that "orders," as understood by them, are nothing more nor less than a superstition? For instance, what would the patrons of the "mass in masquerade" answer to Stanley's direct and emphatic pronouncement: "In the beginning of Christianity there was no such institution as the clergy; it grew naturally out of the increasing needs of the community . . . the intellectual element in religion requires some one to express it, and this, in some form or other, will be the clergy"?[1] Surely if there were no "orders" in the beginning, then a priesthood was no creation of Jesus, his apostles were no priests, they created, therefore, no priests, and a priestly caste grew up as an intrusion in Christendom just as it arose in the religion of the holy Buddha in India, and attempted, though unsuccessfully, to invade the severely simple religion of Mohammed.

The view which ethical religion takes of sacerdotalism is very well known, but it is essential to do more than merely repudiate the notion of priesthood as an integral portion of religion; our duty is also to possess ourselves of the facts of history and criticism so as to satisfy ourselves and others who may need such instruction, that sacerdotalism is not only not ethical, but is anti-Christian, and that the greatest anomaly the world presents to-day is that of the clergymen of the Eastern and Western Churches arrogating to themselves the possession of powers which the founder of their religion and his earliest followers not only never exercised, but of which they had not even a remote conception.

A singular interest has been added to this inquiry by the recently-revived controversy between two of the many Churches into which Christendom is divided on the highly debatable matter of Anglican orders. The said controversy had been in a state of suspended animation from the time of the Stuarts up to the Tractarian movement, when it was partially revived, and a fair crop of literature sprang up around it. It has been reserved, however, for our own days to witness its complete vivification under the auspices of the High Church societies and certain *sagrestani* among "the nobility and gentry" of our day. To the credit of the female sex, we hear of no ladies being *prominently* identified with the movement. Even Oxford, once "the home of lost causes and impossible ideals," concerns itself with these *minutiae* no more. Like the later pantheon of imperial Rome, it offers its impartial hospitality to representatives of every form of orthodoxy and heterodoxy. The shadowy warfare is now waged, apparently, in the London press and magazines, in the bulls of popes and the responsions of archbishops. Of course, the renewed inquiry set on foot by the industry and temerity of Lords Halifax and Nelson—*tanti nominis umbra* surely, in this latter case, to engage itself in such a battle—could have but one ending, namely, the reiterated and emphasised condemnation of our national ecclesiastics as nothing better than mere laymen, and the renewed degradation of the officiating curate to the level of his neighbouring Nonconformist minister who celebrates "the Supper" and preaches in his coat.

The papal representatives in this country have published a rejoinder to the official reply of the Archbishops of Canterbury and York, which, if I may shelter myself behind the authority of the *Times*[2] reviewer, does not err on the side of dignity, moderation and scholarship. It is said to be jaunty, perky, off-hand, suggestive of "the smart evening journalist"—this last is very serious—and, worse than all, it is an appeal, not to theologians or scholars, nor even to thoughtful and instructed men, but "to the gallery".

Who the gallery in this particularly Divine comedy may be I really do not know. I strongly suspect that if the piece were put upon the boards—and everything is now dramatised, from the trials of Satan to the Dreyfus case—the gallery would be the emptiest department of the theatre. And this opinion I am pleased to see confirmed by the closing remarks of the review above noticed, which warns the Christian bishops and pastors of the present day that the comparative merits of one set of "orders" as opposed to those of another set have "little interest and not much meaning for nine Englishmen out of ten".

But what, I think, the average man would be interested to know is whether there be such things as "holy orders" at all. Very many of them are, in this matter, I believe, in the position of those interesting Asiatics who "knew not whether there be such a thing as a Holy Ghost," and I think it will be abundantly easy to show that the ignorance of the ordinary man as to the precise nature of "orders" was shared in also by our Asiatic friends whose existence is noticed in an early chapter of the Acts of the Apostles. We shall therefore proceed to show the groundlessness of the entire controversy from evidence which satisfactorily establishes that the authentic form of Christianity, as fixed by its founder and his followers for two centuries, admits of no such thing as a priesthood in the sense contemplated by the disputants whose wordy warfare has now, we understand, been closed for ever.

To begin, then, whence arose the idea of a priest? What is the meaning of the word? Etymologically, we may take it to be identical with the Saxon word *preost*, which again is doubtless, though it is not admitted on all hands, identical with the Greek *presbys* or elder. A priest, then, originally and literally, signified senior or elder, whether in the family or the State. How an elder came to be associated with religion was in this wise. Every philosopher and anthropologist has been constrained to admit the presence in man of an instinct of unity, impelling him not merely to society or intercourse with his fellows, but to communion with a power unseen. This instinct, as already defined in a former chapter, is religion. Now the initiatory development of this aboriginal instinct was very humble, and if we wish to know what our direct ancestors once were, we need only consult the record of anthropological research among such savages as the Fijians or Tonga Islanders. The shape assumed by religion amongst such people was most probably ancestor or ghost worship. The dead father or chieftain is still seen in the dreams of his children or people, and the mysteriousness of the new shape and presence he assumes excites the awe and reverence which is at the root of the religious habit. The chief becomes the tutelary deity or protector of his tribe, or locality over which he ruled. Other chieftains are added to him in course of time, and soon we have a veritable pantheon of gods, good and evil, whom it is necessary to placate by certain offices and functions, very much as it is necessary to covet the favour of powerful men on earth. Whose duty shall it be to perform such rites? Naturally, it falls to the head of the family and the head of the State. They are the born officers of religious functions, the father for his home circle, the chieftain for his clan or tribe. Thus Livy tells us that Numa, the Roman king, was accustomed to offer sacrifice, but that the increasing cares of State caused him to relinquish the office in favour of specially appointed individuals who were called Flamens, and Mr. McDonald,[3] in his account of the Blantyre negroes, informs us that during the temporary absence of a chief, it devolved upon his wife to take his place at the sacrificial altar. Numberless instances are supplied in such works as Tylor's, Lubbock's, and Spencer's *Ecclesiastical Institutions*, which go to show this primatial or pontifical authority resident in the chief of the State, and the transference of its offices to subordinate people, who gradually and naturally became an official body or caste called priests or elders, as representatives of heads of families, or of the tribe or State.[4] At any rate, however much interested people may be inclined to dispute the lowly origin of religion and worship, the indisputable fact remains that such worship and sacrifice goes on among aboriginal peoples at this very hour, and there is not one shred of evidence, beyond a mistaken prejudice, which goes to show that our religion had any other origin than that.

We may now enter on the further inquiry whether Christianity, meaning thereby the religion personally professed and practised by Jesus of Nazara, was a sacerdotal or sacrificial system in the sense already explained. Such an inquiry necessarily resolves itself into this further one, namely, whether there is any reliable evidence that the founder of the Christian religion was himself a priest, taught a sacerdotal doctrine, or exercised any sacerdotal functions.

Though he died a comparatively young man, if we may believe the gospel narrative, which makes him to have lived either to thirty-one or thirty-three years, though Irenaeus emphatically asserts that he lived to fifty years, we may most assuredly proclaim him a priest in the sense of elder, or leader of men. One whom schools of thought, represented by men so opposed as Mill, Renan, Matthew Arnold, Spinoza, Goethe, Napoleon and Rousseau, conspired to honour must have been indeed a "king of men". But this is not what is meant by the question. By priest we mean here what the ecclesiastic means, namely, one who is set apart by the act of God, signified by some external rite or ceremony, whereby power is conferred to perform certain definite functions impossible to the ordinary man. He alone, in virtue of his consecration, can mediate between man and the Deity, can propitiate him for the sins of men, can forgive those sins, and mechanically communicate holiness by the adoption of a definite ceremony and the pronouncement of a precise formula. Nay, in virtue of his peculiar status, the priest is able to superinduce a physical sanctity in solid and liquid substances, like bread and wine, and quite independently of his own belief, or the belief of the bystanders, or even the recipients, cause those substances to be no longer what to every conceivable physical test they still continue to be, but the body and blood of a man who lived more than 1800 years ago. In a word, a ritual may be described as "a system of consecrated charms or spells, and the priest is the great magician who dispenses them". [5]

What we ask, then, is precisely this: Was Jesus a priest in this sense? Unhesitatingly and most emphatically we reply—and without any fear of serious attempt at refutation—that he was not, and that, in consequence, the whole scheme of sacerdotal religion as prevalent in the Roman and Oriental Christian Churches, and to a moderate extent in the Anglican Church, is entirely baseless, grounded, not on the institution of Jesus their reputed founder, but on an infantine superstition which the third century of Christianity took over from the Jewish and Pagan traditions which had preceded it. Hence the whole protracted controversy, which has set no end of theological hair on end, about the validity of these orders and the invalidity of those, is so much beating the air, because Christianity, as understood and instituted by Christ, knows no place, any more than Buddhism or Mohammedanism, for priest, rite or sacrament.

Let us proceed to offer some evidence for this statement. In the first place, the whole tenor of Christ's life was not that of the priest, but of something entirely different; Christ was a prophet. What is a prophet? We shall very imperfectly appreciate the character of the prophet if we look upon him as nothing more than an historian "for whom God has turned time round the other way," so that he reads the future as if it were the past. Most extraordinary instances of clairvoyance are brought to our notice in which things, eventually realised, turn out to have been previously known, but the clairvoyant is not the prophet. The prophet is the spirit representative of the Supreme Spirit before our own. He is the image—perfected by intercourse with the Unseen—of "the Invisible Goodness". He uses no rites, sacraments or symbols, for he is all that in himself. If his pure, lofty, ennobling life cannot impress the eternal upon the souls of men, then assuredly no bread, wine or oil, can do it.[6] Hence, we see, a prophet is born, not made. No consecration can make one any more than installing a scene painter in the studio of a Raphael could ensure a reproduction of a Transfiguration, or the Madonna di Foligno. And no desecration, no excommunication from church, chapel or sanhedrin can unmake him. The prophet is one of those royal beings who are kings by right Divine, aye and human too, for all fall down instinctively before him. It is the verdict of history that all that is most blessed we owe to the prophets—not to the priests—to Moses, Confucius, Chrishna, Buddha, Socrates, Zoroaster and Christ.

Now, surely no one can seriously question that the life of Christ as described in the gospel narrative is of a pronounced anti-sacerdotal type. He was not of the priestly family, no man laid hands upon him, he never exercised priestly functions. His teaching so directly tended to the disparagement of priesthood as such, that the official hierarchy of his country, quick to perceive it, compassed his death in the interest of their self-preservation. "What do we, for lo! the whole world has gone after him?" His first sermon was the announcement of a prophetic mission. In the synagogue of his own town, among the humble folk who had seen him grow from boyhood to youth and manhood, he made the announcement: "The spirit of the Lord is upon me, because the Lord hath anointed me to preach the gospel to the poor". If he entered the stately courts of the temple, it was to teach rather than to worship, and never to sacrifice. At the close of a day's teaching, he retires to the hillside of Olivet, and feels the Great Presence in the night breeze upon his brow and in the heaven above him as deeply as within the walls of the "Holy Place". It is not, "Lo here, lo there!" for "the Kingdom of God is within you". A priest would have said the Divine Presence is upon the altar, but Christ discerns it always and everywhere. His teaching was almost entirely delivered under the canopy of heaven—on the mount of beatitudes, in a public street, in the market-place, from a fishing boat to crowds upon the strand, in a corn-field, or occasionally in some private dwelling-place. The only invective that broke the calm of his peaceful speech was directed against the ruling sacerdotal influence; he was emphatically a "Prophet of the Most High".

The word *hiereus*, or sacrificing priest, is never once applied to him in the Gospels, and only in one epistle, that to the Hebrews, and there its appearance is not unworthy of our notice. Christ is declared to be a *hiereus*, or priest, *only after* his removal from earth. It is stated that it is an office which did not, which could not have belonged to him while on earth—precisely the point we contend. But how is it that in this epistle he comes to be designated as a priest at all? It was probably due to the exigencies of controversy. The epistle must be looked upon as a polemical pamphlet directed against those Hebrews who refused to embrace the new reform and derided its absence of priest, sacrifice and altar. Conscious that Jesus left no priesthood behind him, that his teaching was anti-sacerdotal and non-sacramental, there was nothing for the writer but to suggest that the great prophet himself was the high priest, the *solitary member of the caste* in the new gospel, and that therewith men are to be satisfied, because more than compensated thereby for the absence of the altar and hierarchy of old. So we have here an unique instance of the exception which proves the rule. Once and once only is the founder of Christianity affirmed to be a priest, and then by an anonymous writer, in a production which the whole Western Church for centuries refused to acknowledge as inspired, and on examination it turns out that by the very nature of the priesthood ascribed to him, such an institution is no longer possible on earth; it is banished for ever into invisibility, and can have no longer any representatives amongst men.

In like manner we find no instance of any attempt on the part of Jesus to make his immediate followers priests. He called them "witnesses," bade them "preach" and "teach". If he told them to baptise, or to break bread in memory of him, we shall soon see that, in the first three centuries of Christian history, his words were emphatically not taken to mean that no one but they, or such as they, could perform these offices. That which men call "the apostolic succession," and to which some of them apparently attach supreme importance, is nothing but a chimera, positively unknown to Jesus or his apostles, and absolutely unintelligible to the Christian Church for more than 200 years. The most profound silence on the whole subject prevails during this period, in vivid contrast with the language held on the subject by subsequent writers. In the face of available, and even readily accessible evidence, it is impossible to maintain that, before the age of Cyprian, the Bishop of Carthage, who flourished about the middle of the third century, there was any such distinction between clergy and laity as the apostolic succession theory maintains to-day. The very names of the clergy, such as deacon, presbyter, and bishop, are lay terms, borrowed from civil not ecclesiastical life. A deacon is a domestic servant; a presbyter, an elder; and a bishop an overseer or bailiff; and in conformity with these names there was no office or function of the Church so exclusively proper to the clergy as not to be capable of performance also by the laity. And if this can be shown, what follows but that the whole conception of "holy orders" is an absolute innovation upon the original teaching of Jesus—a corruption fruitful in disorders, or rather disasters, of the most deplorable character, and at this very hour tending more than any other ascertainable cause to divide man from man, and perpetuate the mischief of religious dissension?

To begin with, then, preaching was indiscriminately permitted in the apostolic times and subsequently. This may be gathered freely from the Acts and Paul's first epistle to the Corinthians, chapter xiv. Moreover, one of the most interesting monuments of the second century is a homily delivered by a layman at Rome, a fragment of which had long been known as the second epistle of Clement,[7] and the remainder of which came to light in 1875 in two forms, a Greek MS. and a Syriac translation. Moreover, the *Apostolical Constitutions,* which are still later—going well into the second century—expressly contemplate preaching by a layman. Dr. Hatch does not hesitate to say that the earliest positive prohibitions of lay preaching were issued solely in the interests of ecclesiastical order, not because there was any inherent right in the priest to teach as opposed to the layman.

Next, in regard to baptism, there need be no hesitation in admitting the capacity of the layman to baptise, because the Church of Rome admits it to-day, nay, it admits that a Mohammedan, or even the heathen Chinaman—if indeed he be such—could lawfully and validly perform that function. This, I submit, is not to be construed as an act of liberality on the Church's part. It is simply the result of the impasse to which it would otherwise be brought by the grotesque teaching that the Deity would condemn everlastingly the soul of an unbaptised infant. This, according to Augustine, being the Christian religion, naturally some loophole had to be fabricated, because priests are not always at hand in moments of emergency, and consequently the validity of lay baptism had necessarily to be recognised.

But there is one office which the Anglican, no less than the Roman Church, would reserve to the priest, and that is the celebration of the Eucharistic Supper.[8] It is abundantly clear to historians that the root-source of the superstitious belief in orders is to be found in the Eucharist and the theories which sprang up in the third century concerning the elements. It cannot be doubted that previously to the age of Cyprian, the communion was held to be what its name designates—an holy assembly, a pledge of unity symbolised by the common partaking of bread and wine after the example of Christ. Now, it is clear from the Ignatian epistles, writings of the second century, whoever may have been their author, that the Christians of those days were accustomed to hold Eucharistic meetings other than those over which a presbyter or elder presided. The practice is indeed reproved by the writer, but in exceeding gentle tones. "Break one bread," says the writer; "be careful to have only one Eucharist"; "let that be the valid Eucharist which is celebrated by the bishop or by some one commissioned by him".

It is surely positively inconceivable that Ignatius of Antioch, or whoever the author of these letters is, can have held the sacramental doctrine subsequently introduced and have used language of such mild remonstrance to the Asiatic Christians he addresses. What would the present occupant of the See of Antioch, of Lincoln, or of Rome say to a number of Christians who assembled together to-day, took bread and wine, and after repeating the Lord's prayer—for they did no more in the early centuries—proceeded to partake of it? Their holy horror is scarcely conceivable. And yet, these lay folk would be the true Christians, not their sacerdotal denunciators. Let us repeat, there was no office open to the priest which was not equally open to the layman. Merely considerations of order and procedure restricted ecclesiastical functions to a particular body or caste of men, and consequently the theory of the essential distinction between priest and layman is not a tenable one because it is none of Christ's making.[9]

It has been remarked that perverse conceptions of the Eucharist were responsible for the equally corrupt teaching about orders. This is the case. Previously to the third century, the Eucharist remained what it had ever been, "the breaking of bread," the commemorative meal. Then there came a change, and men began to read into it a sacrificial meaning and to interpret it as a mystical repetition of the death of Christ. From Cyprian this novel theology apparently passed to Augustine and Ambrose in the fourth century, and thenceforth it became dominant, though by no means universally so, until the eighth and ninth centuries. The rise of Athanasianism in the fourth century, and the abuse of the doctrine of incarnation by that bishop, reacted naturally in the matter of the Eucharist. Christ, who was proclaimed to be the solitary incarnation, the Deity hidden behind a veil of flesh, naturally paved the way for the Eucharist as a sacrament wherein the Deity is hid behind the veil of bread. The one incarnation is, as it were, the complement of the other. Hence, a rigidly literal meaning was given to Christ's utterances about eating his flesh and drinking his blood, and Christians were taught to believe that by the manducation of his bodily frame his holy spirit could be incorporated, as though, for example, a man might hope to become a poet or a sculptor by feeding upon the flesh or bones of a Shakespeare or a Michael Angelo. Only mind can know and receive mind, and it is really difficult to comprehend the grossness of soul which suggests to man the idea that by feasting on the flesh and blood of his God he may hope to become like a God.

It would be just as easy to show that in the matter of church government and discipline everything was, in the early days, on a thoroughly democratic, or representative basis. Power, as in the England of to-day, is recognised to reside in the community, not exclusively in the presbyters. St. Paul's first epistle to the Corinthians recognises this in the matter of the removal of officers. The epistles of Clement and Polycarp recognise the same thing. Bishops are always elected by the people, and the net conclusion therefore is that no such thing as a hierarchy of ordained deacons, priests and bishops was known to Christ, to Paul, or the writers of the first two and a half centuries. The teaching and belief of those days was nonsacerdotal and non-sacramental, and nothing but a superstitious accretion overlaying the original truth can account for the spectacle which vast portions of the Christian world now present, as indeed do vast portions of the Buddhist world. The fate reserved for both these great prophets seems to be identical, the submergence of their pure and elevated ethical teaching beneath an accumulated mass of traditionary and ceremonial law; but here in the West, at all events, there appears to be a well-grounded hope that it is not altogether impossible to get back to Christ and his pure and wholesome teaching. Prophets have arisen in this past century who have far more influence than many priests, and there may be "some standing here" who will witness the close of the reign of the priest and the restoration of the dominion of the prophet.

The priests and scribes sat in the chair of Moses in the days of Christ, and that chair is overturned. No one knows where to look for it. Now we have another priest who sits in Peter's chair, a third who holds Augustine's seat, and a fourth and a fifth who can trace back their priestly ancestry in unbroken line to some era of superstition and decay. The same thing goes on in India and Ceylon, and in Thibet you have the Grand Lamas, to whom successively is united, by a sort of hypostatic union, the holy Spirit himself. Always and everywhere the shadow of the priest, the mystical, magical dispenser of the favours of heaven! We look to the days when religion shall be purified of such conceptions, when no one shall venture to stand between a man and his conscience, or claim to possess powers unattainable by other men, or pretend that the favour of heaven can be purchased by any other means than those indicated by the prophet of old and no less by the conscience of mankind—a life in accordance with righteousness, that is, a life in conformity with the moral law and the example of that supreme among the prophets of the race—Jesus who was called the Christ.

[1] *Christian Institutions*, p. 193.

[2] See *Times*, 5th February, 1898.

[3] Quoted in Spencer's *Ecclesiastical Institutions*.

[4] The appointment of Aaron by Moses, the leader of the Hebrew people, is the exact counterpart of the institution of the Flamens by Numa.

[5] Martineau, *Studies of Christianity*, p. 38.

[6] And, therefore, we note the inconsistency of the sacramentarian theory. It insists on moral goodness in the recipients and ministers of sacraments. But if the rite works of itself, its mechanical performance should be sufficient. But no; goodness is needed to secure any benefit therefrom; and this, of course, is the explanation of the alleged results of the sacraments. The moral goodness of the recipient has already secured the blessing before any rite has been administered.

[7] So that what had been thought to be a papal letter turns out to be a lay homily, showing that a layman could preach as well as a pope in the second century of our era. This suggests the notorious fact that unordained ministers are equally, if not more, successful in awakening ethical and religious emotion than priests and bishops. Nay, women like Catherine of Siena could hold Europe, its kings, and popes spell-bound, when "mere men" were powerless. Has any one in this generation read more powerful appeals to the religious sense than the fragments of the sermons of Dinah Morris in *Adam Bede*, more thrilling descriptions of an unavailing remorse than in the sermon on the text, "Keep innocency, and take heed to the thing which is right, for this shall bring a man peace at the last," which is preached by the agonised minister in *The Silence of Dean Maitland*?

[8] The recent papal rescript on Anglican ordination makes it the test of the comparative value of the rival "orders".

[9] Tertullian in the *De Corona* distinctly declares that though "it is only from the hands of our president we receive the Eucharist, if there be an emergency, a layman may celebrate as well as a bishop". I am indebted to the late Dr. Edwin Hatch for the historical evidence above adduced as to the church practice prevalent in the earliest centuries of Christianity. I would

recommend interested readers to consult his Bampton Lectures, delivered in 1882.

VIII.

PRAYER IN THE ETHICAL CHURCH.

The most important consequence of the new faith that religion is rooted and grounded not in doctrine but in morality, is the belief that the religious instinct grows with the growth and advancement of the moral sense. The old conception that everything religious was revealed once for all 1900 years ago, that it is impious to add to, or modify, the heavenly communication then made, we find ourselves obliged to repudiate in terms. And, hence, we have no creed or articles. We never know when, owing to advancing knowledge, we may be compelled to discard them. The desperate straits to which the Churches and their professional apologists are reduced in their endeavours to reconcile antiquarian statements in Scriptures and theologies with the authenticated facts of mental and physical science, are not such as to encourage us to attempt a definition of the Indefinable, or the comprehension of the Infinite within the exiguous limits of human thought and speech. We are too young by some centuries to so much as think about the formulation of a doctrinal code.

The moral sense, it is abundantly obvious, is growing from day to day. The community herein is the counterpart of the individual. And hence, the moral and religious observances of to-day may become obsolete to-morrow. "The altar-cloths of one generation become the door-mats of the next." Hence, I am full of confidence that though everything may be against us now, one thing is on our side—that is, the future. We saw an illustration of this truth in the history of the relations between the priest and the prophet; we shall witness a further instance of its workings in the history of prayer.

What is the attitude of a human and ethical religion towards that characteristic manifestation of piety which we call prayer? Doubtless its views will be found to diverge notably from those which were prevalent in other days when scientific knowledge was imperfect, and conceptions of man and the Infinite even more inadequate than they admittedly are at present. The origin of prayer is, like the origin of all things terrestrial, extremely humble. When primitive man found himself face to face with the more terrible of the natural phenomena—terrors and portents which he was wholly unable to explain—his only resource was to ascribe their appearance to the agency of beings like himself, though, of course, immeasurably more powerful. These phenomena being often attended by the destruction of the results of laborious industry, and even of human life itself, it became a matter of urgency to devise means whereby the anger of the preternatural powers might be appeased, and a cessation of the successive scourges effected. It was then that man began to offer up entreaty, supplication, petition and prayer to the dread divinities in whose power it was to behave so malevolently towards man and his possessions.

That this account of the matter is not fanciful, the reports of travellers and missionaries in savage lands make certain; and as the inhabitants thereof now are, we certainly once were in our ancestors who dwelt in these northern islands, in the days after the cessation of the glacial periods. There is not one shred of scientific evidence available which would help us to the comforting belief that, however it may be with the Matabele or the Tonga Islanders, the ancestors of Christian England were anything different. That, then, which is called the instinct or habit of prayer, had its origin in the ignorance and superstition of an age which knew nothing of the inviolable reign of law throughout the infinities of the Divine creation, in an age whose religious conceptions were as gross as their scientific ideas were absurd.

Now, the unscientific and unphilosophical taint, which marked the earliest heavenward cries of terrified man, has clung to the petitions which he offers up at this hour for material favours and blessings. At the close of a prolonged drought, the Archbishops of Canterbury and York compose a prayer for rain, and as a drought cannot last for ever, rain does eventually come, and the same dignitaries then order a prayer to be offered up in thanksgiving. But does any one really suppose that the natural order of the phenomena has been altered at the request of the clergy by an Almighty mind? It were preposterous, grotesque and irreverent, in the highest degree to think so. And the proof that it is preposterous is seen in the fact that prayers are no longer offered up for the advent or cessation of the effects of phenomena whose causes have been scientifically determined. Thus, in mediaeval days, man placed bells high in the steeples of his churches to deafen the demons who caused the storms of thunder and lightning which destroyed his property. At this day one may read the inscriptions on the bells which testify to the belief of the time. But as soon as the lightning rod was discovered by Franklin, and its absolute ability to conduct the electric current to the soil, bells were no longer requisitioned as antidotes to storms, and prayers and litanies ceased to be sung to petition the Divine clemency against the effects of the weather. In the same way an outbreak of cholera or diphtheria once sent people in their thousands to the churches and chapels; now it sends them to the drains, and while prayers proved but a poor prophylactic against epidemics, the most pious credulity now places unbounded faith in a sanitary system approved by a first-class surveyor. Can there be any possible doubt that, when the laws of meteorology are as well known as those which govern the tides or the thunderbolts, the archbishops will cease to order any more prayers for the purpose of controlling the elements?

Then, there is another aspect of petitionary prayer which demands a passing notice. It actually represents the Supreme Being as an individual who will interfere with what are manifestly natural laws to suit the convenience or even the whim of the votary; and worse than that, that the course of events will be so ordered as to meet the requirements of the individual supplicant, to the exclusion of the needs, the convenience or circumstances, of numberless other human beings who may be seriously incommoded, possibly even wronged, if the first votary's supplications are granted. It is of little avail to have recourse to the mechanical theory that infinite power is capable of so adjusting matters as to satisfy everybody. These are words and phrases more sonorous than satisfactory. When, for instance, war breaks out between two Christian powers, the Almighty is at once petitioned to crown both combatants with victory, and that done, victory is always assumed by the conqueror to mean that the Divine blessing has been with him to the exclusion of his adversary. But the remarkable fact to the impartial observer uniformly is, that victory always rests with those who have made the best preparations, conducted the campaign in the most skilful manner, and fought with the greatest determination, or as Napoleon curtly put it, that as far as he could see, Providence was always on the side of the strongest battalions.

I recently heard read a lady's letter in which she poured forth her most fervent gratitude to heaven because her husband had been elected to a certain influential position over the heads of seventy competitors. Unless sixty-nine other equally desirable posts were magically created by Divine power, it seems difficult to understand, on the supposition that the election was the arbitrary act of God, how the claims of all were satisfied in this individual instance. The truth is that the prayer of petition ought instantly to cease as infantine, irrational, and irreverent. The serious man cannot bring himself to offer up vocal prayers for temporary or spiritual benefits, which are manifestly attainable by the capacity of man's natural powers, or which cannot be heard without a selfish indifference to the equal rights and claims of others. And, therefore, no petitionary prayers find a place in the service of the ethical Church. The God whom we recognise is the "Mind who meditates in beauty and speaks only in law"; the "beneficent Unity," the "beautiful Necessity"; the law which is not intelligent, but Intelligence. It were as impious to pray for an infraction of the natural laws of Divine ordaining as it were foolish to wish that the law of gravitation were suspended to gratify a passing need or whim. In the Talmud there is a prophetic intimation of the religion which asks no favours, but prays by living the moral life. It foretells the day when prayer shall cease in the Jewish Church, and thanksgiving only be henceforth heard. This exactly expresses what we feel should be the attitude of the reverent man in the silence of the Great Presence—his life an attestation of his recognition of what he owes to the Being whose nature he shares.

But, it will doubtless be urged, prayers are answered even when offered for purely temporary blessings, or at any rate, numberless men and women contend that they have been so answered in their own experience. Members of the more emotional forms of Nonconformity are especially emphatic in their testimony to the efficacy of prayer, though I doubt not that their more educated ministers would hesitate to commit themselves to the belief in its more extreme forms. Mr. Armstrong certainly disavows it for the Unitarian body, a Church always to be held in reverence as having done more to rationalise religion in this country and America than any other agency we could indicate. But what are we to say to such testimonies? This, that the prayers have been answered by the supplicants themselves, when even, indeed, we have not to deal with a matter of mere coincidence. But, I would expressly guard against the inference being drawn, that I question the

Divine Personality. I lay down no dogmatic statements as to the efficacy of vocal prayers. What I do say is, that all I know of God as revealed in nature and law forbids me to entertain the notion that the order he has seen fit to establish is to be capriciously altered at the request of any of his creatures. It is not irreverence, but a sense of reverence which prohibits me from believing that the Being whose presence and power are revealed in the least as in the greatest of the phenomena of nature, is open to arbitrarily interfere with the established course of things because an individual or a score of individuals wish it.

But what of the alleged answers to prayers which are held to establish its efficacy? I unhesitatingly ascribe the results to increased activity, more resolute determination, on the part of the natural will of the votary. Let a man, for example, become convinced that the crisis of his life has arrived, that a certain policy must be at once adopted, a certain post secured, or an examination passed, and the natural bending of the energies in a given direction redoubles his ordinary powers. If a post has to be obtained and influence is necessary, he prosecutes a more resolute canvass; if an examination must be passed, a degree secured, he reads with increased application, and, as a matter of course, he succeeds. If, in the meantime, he has had recourse to prayer, his womankind, or possibly he himself, will ascribe the entire results to that agency, while the results are altogether due to his own persistent efforts. *He has answered his own prayers.* Does the most pious individual believe, if all efforts were remitted, or no exceptional energy put forth by the individual in question, but the whole matter left entirely "in the hands of God," as the phrase runs, that any successful results would have ensued? Not one. And hence those axioms which the common-sense, even of the most credulous, adopts as true, namely, that, "Heaven only helps those who help themselves," or, as another pious recommendation goes, "Pray as though everything depended on God, *act as though everything depended on yourself*". What wonder, when this advice is followed out to the letter, that we are overwhelmed with assurances that prayers have been answered, when a man is appointed to a sinecure or has obtained a life-pension? What one would like to ask is this: Do these credulous people suppose that the event would have been otherwise, had the young candidate not prayed? Do they suppose that the Deity would positively have snatched away the prize at the last moment, and given it to another, simply because he had not been consulted in the matter? If they do, then we must confess our ideals of the Divine are very different from theirs.

Powers are given to man for one purpose—that he may use them—and to us it is wholly irrational to suggest that what is given with one hand is to be taken away with the other, because the formality of supplication is not employed when anything of moment is to be put into execution. The notion that intelligence was put in man only to be shattered, a will given him only to be forthwith distorted by passion or blinded by ignorance, and that "there is no health in us" unless we abase ourselves to the dust and proclaim our utter worthlessness, is to men and women of this time wholly inconceivable. That nothing ethically valuable can be accomplished except after instant prayer, or after copious outpourings of Divine grace, that the curse of absolute sterility is upon all our attempts to conform to the dictates of the moral law, unless God be with us in prayer, is henceforth an impossible theology.

Tell us that the man and the world are dependent at every instant of time on the sustaining and prolonged creative act of the Infinite Being, and we are one with you, nay, we probably go beyond you. "He is not very far from any one of us" means more to the scientific philosopher than to the mediaeval theologian. But spare us the repetition of those stale legends that man was made and unmade in the space of a few moments, and that ever since the manducation of the forbidden fruit his powers have withered, and that there is no remedy available for their recovery but incessant prayer and sacramental ordinances. Our reading of history is exactly the reverse. With the progress of time we discern the advance of man, and with the diminution of sacerdotalism and a mechanical religion we think we note an accelerated progress; that in those countries in which men are nobly self-reliant, and look *within* instead of *without* for the source of their inspiration and power, the course of moral life takes a higher turn; that in proportion as men are true to themselves and the powers of their own being, they ascend in the scale of moral perfection. We think that to teach a man to look without him for assistance is to cripple half his powers, to make him unlearn the grand gospel of self-reliance, to loosen the fibres of his moral being, and thereby to check his individual progress.[1]

It must have been some such conviction as this which led the late Master of Balliol to say that the longer he lived the less he prayed, but the more he thought. Precisely; it is not irreverence but a deepening reverence for the Divine powers within us, which shames us into trusting them when anything great is to be done. What god are you praying to, we ask in dismay, when you lift up your hands and your eyes, or turn to east or west, or kneel or lie? Is there any god in the wastes of infinity, in a sunstar, a swarm of worlds, who is not in that miraculous soul of yours? Is there aught anywhere greater than a son of God? Is a stone, a star, a heaven studded with infinite glories, a greater place than your eternal soul? Then look within you. Speak with yourself, commune with your own heart, summon up the irresistible energies of your nature and nothing shall be impossible to you. This is "the prayer of faith" that never shall, that never can, go unanswered, the concentration of the myriad energies of our souls to meet an attack, to prosecute an enterprise, to overcome obstacles, aye, to make our lives sublime with a heroism that men shall call divine. "The less I pray, but the more I think!" Aye, it is not prayer in the old sense, the cry of the soul that believes itself craven, weak and wanton, because it has always been told so by blind guides; it is not this aimless outpouring of energy directed towards a Divinity in the skies, when the very Life and Mind Divine are the endowments of every rational creature, that has made man great; but thought, concentration, the serious, resolute application of the powers that man does possess, the bending of the iron energies to the accomplishment of the individual task—this it is which has "conquered kingdoms, wrought righteousness, obtained the promises," riveted man's dominion over nature and made him what he was intended to be—the crown and glory of the universe.

And at this point we may make a further suggestion towards explaining the genesis and the continued maintenance of vocal prayer as a part of religious worship. The practice would seem to be due not merely to ignorance or disregard of the obvious law of cause and effect, by which material phenomena are necessarily controlled, but to less worthy conceptions of the Divine Mind governing all things. The Deity of the Christian and Mohammedan worlds is a Being eternally dissevered from a world which he has by an omnipotent effort evoked from nothingness—a conception now regarded as impossible. Consequently, while God is in his high heaven, surrounded by his court, the world holds on its courses, and is periodically corrected by special interferences, generally said to be due to the intervention of prayer. Thus, the grand historical evolution, which caused the Roman Empire to appear at the close of the three great Eastern Empires, and that monument of human genius itself to ultimately collapse and make way for the nations which now constitute modern Europe, in no wise strikes Augustine, or any orthodox teacher, even of to-day, as the outcome of purely natural forces and influences—the action and reaction of powers wholly human—but as part of a Divine scheme, which was foreordained for the purpose of founding the Christian Church. This, in briefest outline, is the famous argument of "The City of God," the first Christian attempt at a philosophy of history. Everything mapped out by

Divine ordinance, and men moved like puppets to accomplish the scheme. Attila the Hun appears at the gates of Rome, in the fifth century, and threatens to sack it, and thereby delay the execution of the plan, and prayer averts the disaster. In all moments of danger, threatened catastrophe, public or private, the doctrine inculcated was recurrence by prayer to the external Deity, who would so modify things by his omnipotent power, as to reconcile the interests of all concerned. I do not think it can be said that such a frame of mind is distinctive of the Protestant of to-day, certainly not of the instructed Protestant, who may acquiesce in the vicarious repetition of certain formulas by his clergyman on Sunday morning, but would certainly not in practice endorse the theory that Divine intervention might be called in at any moment by prayer. But it is the attitude of the Roman and Greek Churches, as it is of the Mohammedan religion, and doubtless of the less educated in the sects of Nonconformity.

Now this conception of Divinity is Oriental, whence indeed our current religion arose. It represents the Supreme Being as an aged man clothed in flowing robes, his hair "white as wool," seated on a golden throne and ceaselessly adored by myriads of voices who sing day and night, Holy, Holy, Holy, or Hallelujah. It is the conception of a Divinity who existed an eternity in the solitude of his own kingdom, amid silences unbroken by any voice, who suddenly comes to the determination to create worlds and man out of nothing, and orders men to pray and to praise him. He is angry if they do not; he is "a jealous God," and will punish those who offend him "to the fourth generation". He is sorry he has made man and proceeds to destroy him, and then subsequently regrets that decision. In a word, the God of the Hebrew tradition, whom the Christian Church still popularly preaches, is in reality a magnified copy of an Oriental Sultan, whose tastes and proclivities are such as the *Arabian Nights* has familiarised us with—greedy of praise, adulation and homage, cruel and vindictive to those who refuse their worship and adoration.

Now this Orientalism is no longer tolerable in the eyes of thoughtful people. We cannot conceive that the Infinite Being should find pleasure in hearing all day and night how wonderful he is, and how miraculous his works. It is not easily intelligible how services and litanies of "praise" can be acceptable to the Creator when they would certainly be nauseous to the best men on earth. Jesus openly reproved one who praised him as "the good master". "Call no man good," he said: "God only, he is good." Wellington's reply to the famous individual who claimed to have "saved the life of the saviour of Europe" is too well known to repeat. The truth is, that these prayers and chants are offered up not for God's sake, but for *ours*. They are a relief to the heart surcharged with religious emotion, the outcome of the vehement impulse of the soul towards communion with the Life of its life. Speaking reverently, prayer and praise are like a lover's protestations, which are not an act of adulation at the shrine of his mistress, but an irresistible unburdening of the greatness of the emotion that fills his heart. But no lover could speak from his soul in a public place, in the sight or hearing of other men. Solitude, silence, "the element in which everything truly great is made," is needed above all else, that the soul may find adequate utterance for thoughts so sublime.

And, therefore, Jesus warned man to pray in his own chamber, in secret, the lonely soul bared in the presence of the Alone, "to the Father which seeth in secret". Hence no sound of spoken prayer is heard at our services. The deed is too solemn. Nevertheless, the whole object of the series of acts which are done is to suggest, to create, first thought, and then emotion, after the manner of the Hebrew psalmist, who sang "In the midst of my thoughts shall a fire flame forth". The *hymns* are chosen with the idea, not of praising the Almighty, who needs no such praises, but of filling our souls with a sense of the unearthly beauty of the moral life, of the life perseveringly devoted to high ideals of self-culture and human service, and thereby lifting our souls to thoughts of that fair world of the Ideal in which such conceptions are eternally realised. Likewise the *readings* set before us the burning words of first one and then another prophetical soul to deepen in our own the conviction of the seriousness of life, its far-reaching responsibilities, the realisation of the boundless capacities for good or evil which man has within him, and the utter worthlessness of all things on this earth compared with character, integrity, the perfection of the will by conformity with the moral law.

In the midst of such influences by which we are surrounded during the hour, all too brief, which we devote to the world of the Ideal on one day out of seven,[2] it is hoped that thoughts will sometimes burn in many hearts, that reverence, awe, fear, regrets for the past, fervent resolutions for the future, hope, aspiration, and love; in a word, all the sanctified emotions of the human heart, which together melt into the supreme emotion of religion, will sometimes arise to sternly rebuke the selfish life, shame us out of our moral lethargy, and comfort those whose one solace is that their honour is intact, though misfortune has stricken them in mind or body, or robbed them of the goods of earth, or the cheer and comfort of friendship and of love. It is hoped that the influence of what is said and done then will endure beyond the hour of our meeting, and fill some other moments of our lives when we are, as we should be, at seasons, alone—alone with ourselves, and *therefore* alone with God, in solemn communion with the Soul who is the soul in us, and who asks for no articulate voice of prayer, but only that our life in every word and deed should be worthy of our exalted nature. Life is prayer. Conduct is sacrifice. Morality is religion.

> When I am stretched beneath the pines,
> When the evening star so holy shines,
> I laugh at the lore and the pride of man,
> At the sophist schools and the learned clan;
> For what are they all in their high conceit,

When man in the bush with God may meet?
    —EMERSON.

[1] See the concluding words of Emerson's essay on "Self-Reliance".

[2] The Ethical Religion Society meets weekly on Sunday mornings.

IX.

THE ETHICAL ASPECT OF DEATH.

There is a common but none the less erroneous impression amongst those who walk and worship in the old ways, that the newer forms in which the religious sentiment expresses itself are insensible to the more solemn aspects of life, its sins and sorrows, its disappointments and disillusionment, and most of all to the final catastrophe which men call death. Ours, they would impress upon us, is a fair weather creed, good enough when all goes well, but painfully inadequate in the storm and stress which the inevitable trials of existence inflict upon us. Sorrow, they impressively warn us, is ever the rock upon which all such systems must split.

Now, to say nothing of the obvious reflection that what we now call the old, that is, the orthodox ways, are in reality exceedingly new, and that even the "chosen people," or their immediate predecessors, were left wholly destitute by the Deity of any such comforts as are held so indispensably necessary to a well-ordered existence—to say nothing of this, the argument, if worth anything, would go to show that the religion which offered most consolation was the true one; and since no traveller ever returns from that bourne, so near and yet so far, to advise us of the truth or falsity of these ultra-mundane comforts, we seem compelled to hesitate more than ever before we forsake that sturdy and plain-spoken guide called reason, whom we as confidently follow in the region of religion as in the business of everyday life. The Society for Psychical Research has some remarkable evidence to offer, apparently establishing to physical demonstration that *the* man [Transcriber's note: the *man*?] in us does not die but lives, and communicates with his fellows after the final fact of this earth called death. But, however this may be, and we are not called upon now to offer any opinion on these matters, the so-called revelations are wonderfully silent on those topics which sentimentarians apparently erect into the supreme test of a religion's truth or falsity. As far as one may judge, the departed appear to be occupied with nothing more sublime than filled their thoughts during this present sphere; in fact, as is well known, they often appear to exhibit a painful declension in moral life and to have lost immeasurably in character by their passage from this stage of being to the unknown land beyond the grave.

Reason, therefore, being in no position to settle the rival claims of the physical delights of the Mohammedan paradise, the comparatively insipid ideal of the Apocalypse, and "the nameless quiet" of the Buddhist Nirvana, feels compelled to pass them all by and to hold that of the invisible universe we are painfully ignorant, and that the only deathless reality is the will of man conformed to the great obedience of the moral law. It believes that the test of a system is not what it promises but what it performs, and we may take it as an absolutely certain thing that if any of the "systems" of our day secured palpably higher ethical results amongst its adherents, the world would flock to that Church forthwith. As Augustine says, "no one loves the devil," which, being ethically interpreted, means no one wants to be bad, and if any ecclesiastical corporation, by an appeal to history or to present and urgent visible facts, could justify its claims to successfully strengthen man's oftentimes rebel will in the pursuit of the great ideal, men would follow it to the world's end, such is the power of truth and goodness over the human heart. But the truth is, no such agency has ever been discovered. In the sixteenth century the Council of Trent was summoned "to reform the

Church in its head and members," a plain confession of ethical failure. Do men suppose that Luther, or a whole synod of monks, could have torn Europe in pieces in about a score of years, when Anglicans have been debating auricular confession and the eastward position for the last fifty, unless the Continent had undergone a moral *débâcle*? Luther's paltry diatribes about indulgences would have left men as cold as stone; it was the fervour of the ethical enthusiast thundering against immoralities in high places which rent the Christian Church in twain by the most violent and widespread schism it had ever known.

No, the test of a thing is not what it promises but what it does. *Exitus acta probat*. And if the enlightened men and women of our time are disposed less and less to rely upon creeds as a basis of religious communion, it is because they see that whatever the future life may have in store for mankind, they cannot better prepare for it than by living worthily in this.

But as evidence that they who follow the ethical obedience are in no wise insensible to the sterner aspects of life, we shall now pass on to say what in our judgment should be the religious attitude of man face to face with the inevitable certainty of death.

If we pause one moment to reflect on the physical aspect of death, it would only be to remark that it is as natural an occurrence as birth. In fact, as is obvious to the most superficial mind, birth and death are inextricably interwoven. The great life of the worlds is so one, so powerful, so omnipresent, that nothing can so utterly pass away as to give birth to nothing—no, not even the cremated remains which are blown to the four winds. The theory that death is a non-natural occurrence arbitrarily inflicted by the Deity in his anger at Adam's disobedience is no longer taught even in the nursery, because aeons upon aeons before man's advent hither death reigned supreme over sentient existence, and the bones of the doomed are in our museums to attest the fact. Nay, we have recovered the ice-embedded body of the mammoth, its stomach filled with undigested food, food it ate as far back as the glacial period, by which it was overtaken and frozen in its ice grave 200,000 years ago. The Roman sentinel, overwhelmed where he stood by the lava of Vesuvius, defiant of disaster in his inflexible devotion to duty, is not a surer proof of the natural fact of death than the mammoth that died in Alaska before man's appearance on the earth. The law of growth is the law of death. Life begins, it increases, it reaches its meridian, it begins to waver and then steadily to decline, till at length the bodily frame dissolves, and then—

> That which drew from out the boundless deep
> Turns again home.

It is so with all things, from a fungus to a giant of the forest, from a stone to a cluster of stars whose light takes 4000 years to reach us. It is only a question of time when our own sun shall set in impotence and rise again no more. All things are passing away, everything is unstable, change is at the heart of all. How solemn, how true the words, whose melancholy haunts the more the memory dwells on them: "this world passeth away and the desire thereof, but he that doeth the Divine will endureth for ever"! As we said, the one changeless thing, beyond the doom of sun-stars and swarms of worlds, is the will of man nobly submissive to the Great Obedience of the Supreme Law—the Law of Justice and of Truth. That alone can never die.

Let us turn now to the ethical and religious aspect of that which we have seen to be in itself so natural, so inevitable.

In the first place, we conceive that it in no wise interrupts the progress of the individual life. Certainly the conditions under which existence maintains itself in that other state must be far other than those which obtain here, for there man is destitute of his bodily environment. The conditions of such a life are wholly unpicturable, wholly unimaginable, but not *inconceivable*. These are high matters, like the truths of sublimest philosophy, wherein it is impious to intrude with so inferior a faculty as imagination, and demand that an image or representation of a bodiless existence be presented to it. What picture does man make for himself of the force of gravitation, nay of the force which drives the crocuses out of the soil in spring? It is enough to *know* that the force is there; it is enough to know that a man's body is not his *self*. Surely every one who reflects must be conscious that his body is *his*, just like his clothes; and therefore not *he*, any more than the raiment wherewith he is covered. Foolish, then, is it to ask for pictures like children; let us be satisfied to know with the reason, which we alone of all earth-born creatures possess, that the body is not *we* but *ours*, and that we are not mere ephemerals, but are "going on and still to be".

Now these words of Tennyson exactly express our ethical teaching, that man is "ever going on and still to be," and that death, so far from putting a stop to the eternal progress, is but a stage, an incident in the journey, possibly—for we know so little of these matters—a very insignificant one. The theory commonly inculcated, certainly commonly held, is that the fact of death ushers in a perfect transformation scene, more wonderful than anything thought of or devised by man, nor should we be accounted irreverent did we describe the language of the book of Revelation as pantomimic in the exuberance of its splendour. All sorrow is supposed to cease as if by magic, the sun shines perpetually, it is eternal noon; the home of the blessed is a wondrous city, built four-square, whose streets are of pure gold, whose rivers are of crystal, and whose foundations are laid in precious stones. Sweetest songs of earth resound in the heavenly courts; yea, even musical instruments are there, and life would appear to be one prolonged religious service. Into this celestial blessedness departed souls enter new-born, and take their allotted places once and for ever; they never apparently move from them; they grow no better; there is no room for further development, nor possibility of deterioration, but a fixed and immovable moral status is, to all appearances, arbitrarily imposed upon them for evermore. The impression one gathers is, therefore, of a large and glorified amphitheatre, tiers rising above tiers into infinity, seats along them, each of which is tenanted by an individual elect spirit whose merits are precisely proportioned to its place.

Now that existence prolonged, I will not say into eternity, but into a week is the very reverse of inspiring. Of course, we are aware that Dean Farrar has as effectually explained away the Orientalisms of the Christian heaven as the Paganisms of the orthodox hell; we are ready to believe that the Apocalypse—which is held now not to be a Christian book at all, but a Jewish composition, edited and amended by a Christian hand—sets forth only figures and types of the great supernal blessedness. This we know, but our difficulty is not with the form but with the content, that is, with that which these hyperboles symbolise. It is fairly inconceivable to us that a matter which, according to the Churches, merely concerns the body, soon to be resolved into its component gases, should exercise so miraculous a transformation on the soul, or the real man. *He* did not die; his body did, and yet they would have us believe that that mere physical occurrence, that catastrophe of flesh and blood, means the subsequent and eternal stagnation of all psychical life; that men either go forthwith into scenes with which ninety out of a hundred would be wholly unfamiliar, or are thrust headlong into a subterranean locality called Sheol, or the grave in Hebrew, the English equivalent of which is hell, the only difference being that, whereas the good can grow no better, the wicked can and do grow worse.

Doubtless, I shall be reminded that these teachings do not occur explicitly in the Thirty-nine Articles, any Church Confession, or a Papal Decree. That may very well be so, as regards them all, but there can be no doubt that the main assertion is accepted as dogmatically true by all Christian Churches—namely, that a wonderful and searching change does occur at the moment of death, whereby "the time of probation," as it is called, comes to an end, and all possibility of further "merit before God," or, as we should say, of ethical advancement, relentlessly cut off. To quote a letter of Cardinal Newman's, written in 1872 to the Rev. W. Probyn-Nevins, and published subsequently by him—in the *Nineteenth Century* of May, 1893—"The great truth is that death ends our probation, and *settles our state for ever*, that there is no passing over the great gulf". Amidst much that is uncertain, for instance, as to whether real devils are in hell, a real fire, and whether it be bright or dark, whether the appalling torments are ever mitigated, say on certain feasts of the Christian Church, such as Christmas Day and Easter, or whether eventually the pains ultimately die completely away and thus usher in that "happiness in hell" in which Mr. Mivart is, or was, so deeply interested five years ago—amidst all these highly debatable points, Newman pronounces one thing certain, that "death ends our probation," that "there is no passing over the great gulf".

Now, whence did he learn this strange teaching? How is he dogmatically certain of that one thing, while all the rest is in a haze? From stray texts, such as, "Whether the tree falleth to the north or the south, in whatsoever place it shall fall, there shall it lie"; or, from the parable of wise and foolish virgins, some of whom happened to be asleep, and awoke at the critical hour to find that during the long night-watch for the bridegroom their store of oil had become exhausted? Surely tropes and parables are a highly insecure foundation whereon to build such a momentous teaching. Certainly, it is gravely questionable whether any direct statement in the Hebrew or Christian writings can be adduced to support the common notion that bodily dissolution is a spiritual reagent, and *ipso facto* seals the destiny of a spiritual essence. Vast numbers of even Anglicans repudiate the notion in the name of theology and religion. We repudiate it in the name of reason, which was put into us for no other purpose, we know well, than to judge not only the statements Churches put forth, but the sacred documents on which they build them. We repudiate the notion in the name of that reason which shows us that the Infinite Mind, whose light and life we share, was millions of years preparing this earth for man's habitation, aeons of time so fashioning the course of things that a body might be prepared in which that mind which we call soul might energise; aeons of time so ordering the course of events that man should emerge one day from the savagedom and animalism of the past to enter upon the path of a progress which we believe to be endless. I say the reason which demonstrates this to us with a certitude which not the most intolerant bigotry dares to question to-day, tells us also that it is wholly preposterous that all that is left to man wherein to work out his own individual moral progress is the brief span of threescore years and ten, that after these days "few and evil," the chapter is closed, the book sealed for ever, and the status of man inexorably and unalterably determined.

I frankly avow I would as soon believe the Buddhist *Jataka* as such a wholly irrational account of the ways of God with man. Just think of the palaeolithic man, who had no glimmering of moral discernment; think of the cave-men whose skulls we possess in scores, that bear eloquent testimony to their deplorable degradation—think of such creatures dying, and their mental and moral status stereotyped for ever. "Death ends our probation!" A precious revelation this! Where and what are these men now? When Newman visited Greece in the thirties what impressed him, or rather oppressed him, as he stood above the glorious bay of Salamis, over which

Those who witnessed the recent revival of *Hamlet*—a revival which it would appear is destined to be historic—cannot have failed to notice how the great master of song permits himself to express the perverse conception that death is synonymous with everlasting moral stagnation. Hamlet steals into his murderous uncle's apartment, sword in hand, but discovering the criminal upon his knees, forbears to strike then, lest somehow his devotions should save him from his doom. No, he will wait until the miserable creature is off his guard, so that death may overtake him at a moment when no prayer or cry for mercy is possible. As though a momentary act could undo the mischief of years! As though a man is in himself any different after years, of crime because he utters a sudden cry for mercy! And, as though by killing him at an opportune moment, Hamlet could damn his soul for ever! And it will be noted, moreover, that the ghost emphasises the treachery of which he has been the victim, in that he was sent into eternity "unhouseled, unaneled," as though momentary acts can make up for years wasted and misspent. As well might one scatter one's fortune in luxury and riotous living, and resolve to win it all back in a moment, as misuse these glorious powers of mind and will we bear within us, turn them to evil, steep them in iniquity, and then think to suddenly turn and by a single act bend them successfully to the arduous service of the good. This is stern teaching, but it is the truth; and a mercy would it be, a mercy would it have been for us all in the days of our youth, if instead of the too frequent insistence on the doctrine of the forgiveness of sin, the doctrine of compensation and retribution, as taught by Ralph Waldo Emerson, had been instilled into our hearts. "Ye shall not go forth until ye have paid the last farthing," is the teaching. Dare to break those solemn laws, to pervert these mysterious powers we possess, Amen, Amen, we cannot escape retribution; we cannot go forth until we pay the last farthing.

And this last thought prepares for the statement of our view of the attitude a rational religion takes up in the solemn presence of death. "Stoicism shall not be more exigent," said Emerson of the new Church. We take no lax view of life and its responsibilities, but we refuse to magnify death into the one thing worth living for or thinking about. *Homo liber de nulla re minus quam de morte cogitat.* We do not set about digging our graves, we do not carry our coffins about with us, still less do we sleep in them—a gruesome practice which has attracted some fanatical folk. To us, death is a fact, not an effect, an incident as natural as birth, in no wise affecting the real, the spiritual, man. We therefore utterly disavow all sympathy with the groundless assumption that a magical change comes over the psychical powers of a man at that supreme moment, whereby he can do no more good, but may harden into a more hopeless reprobate. The notion that a judgment of the soul takes place, as in the hall of Osiris, of Egyptian mythology, at the instant of dissolution, whereby the destiny of the individual is sealed for ever, we repudiate in terms. Man is judged, not then, but at every moment of his life. "The moral laws vindicate themselves" without the intervention of any external tribunal. And, therefore, the eternal progress of the man in us is maintained uninterruptedly across the gloomy chasm of death, under other circumstances, no doubt, but still it is the same ceaseless approach towards the Infinite Ideal, the same untiring journey along "the everlasting way". All are in that "way," we may be sure, even those whom we foolishly deem hopelessly reprobate. Something can be made of those failures of men, for

> After last returns the first, though a wide compass
> round be fetched;
> What began best can't end worst, nor what God once
> blest prove accurst.

But such men, the Neros, Caligulas, the Wainwrights and Palmers of all ages and nations, are but a fractional, an infinitesimal, element in the great human family. *Sanabiles fecit nationes super terram.* "He hath made earth's peoples to be healed;" they shall redeem *themselves* one day. The moment of awakening comes sooner or later to all; there is an unextinguished capacity for good under the sores and scars of the most dissolute life, and we may believe that awakening comes when the spirit enters new-born, as it were, into a world where the illusions of the flesh, the deceptions of the sense, obtain no more.

There are no final, irredeemable failures. The Divine in man must emerge one day; its glory pierce through the gloom of his sin and shame, and transfigure him anew after the beautiful and pathetic image of the holy Christ in the legend,[1] whose closing days on earth, they say, were illumined by one supreme wonder—his face calm and blissful, glowing radiant like the glory of a setting sun, his very raiment turned white like the driven snow. A beauteous imagery! But there was no external transfiguration. It was but a type of the radiant purity within; a witness to the "beauty of holiness". It was an emblem of what all may be in some far-off day, when the lowliest amongst us learns to follow the Christs, the blessed company of all elect souls, in the way which begins and ends in the eternal righteousness.

[1] In the same way the Buddha was "transfigured". See Doane's *Bible Myths*.

X.

THE ETHICAL ASPECT OF WAR.

An idealism such as that which substantially identifies religion with morality, is suitably occupied, as occasion offers, in the discussion of those questions of public interest which have an immediate bearing on the well-being of communities. In this respect it departs markedly from the attitude taken up by those Churches, which afford little or no guidance on such matters, probably because it is felt by priests and prelates that their functions are rather of an ultra-mundane character, and that their most important duty is to prepare humanity for the enjoyment of another life after this unsatisfactory stage has passed. Hence the sharp line of distinction they draw between the Church and the world, the one the kingdom of saints, the other "lying" hopelessly "in wickedness". Hence, again, their distinction of "holy days" and secular days, Sunday being devoted to religious exercises, while the remaining six days are presumably to be occupied in wholly secular enterprise. The distinction affects our very attire. Religious rites being of a totally different character from the duties we accomplish during the week, there is nothing for it but to don "our blacks," to quote the language of a current popular play, and enact subsequently the ceremonial described as the church parade. It is the same feeling which causes the average Englishman to lapse into a sort of funereal solemnity at the very mention of the word religion, or of anything allied to it. The divorce of religion from ordinary life could not be more plainly indicated than by such phenomena as we have noticed.

It is, of course, one of the main objects of our movement to show the falsity of this distinction between the Church and the world, between religion and morality. We submit that it is not the institution of the founder of Christianity, but of his later followers. The Church of Christ meant the assemblage of men *as men, as citizens*. The entry thereto was not by the magical washing away of an imaginary birth-sin, but through the natural and beautiful sacrament of human birth. The world is the Church, and the Church is the world, and the "living stones" out of which "the kingdom of heaven" is built here on earth are precisely the stones out of which the civil commonwealth arises. There is nothing secular, nothing profane, but from first to last the life of every man, from the miraculous moment of his conception to the closing of his eyes in bodily death, and beyond death, through the perfecting of him by an ever-increasing approximation to the standard of all moral perfection, everything is religious, sacred, divine. The Church is nothing but an ethical society, co-extensive with the race, and it is for the realisation of this ideal that the ethical movement is working, to show men that religion is morality, is life.

This preamble, then, may serve as a justification for introducing here such a subject as war. The Christian Churches, with one single exception, that of the Quakers, vouchsafe no guidance whatsoever on the moral aspects of this question. On the contrary, they rather suggest that it is a highly moral proceeding, for their ministers pray to their Deity for the success of their country's arms, and sing their *Te Deums* over the mangled corpses of the vanquished. An archbishop in Spain offered to guarantee the harmlessness of every American bullet, and unctuous prayers were reported in the newspapers of last spring as emanating from Transatlantic pulpits. Indeed, it would be difficult, if not impossible, to imagine what the supreme court of their heaven must be, the perplexities of patron saints and angels, and ultimately of their Deity himself, in face of the immoral mingling of bloodshed and religion which went on during the recent Spanish-American war. But the Churches, Catholic and Protestant alike, see none of the impiety which is so revolting to moral men and women, who to their lasting advantage have emancipated themselves from ecclesiastical guidance. On the contrary, the public in America which looks for moral inspiration to clergymen, is fed upon this sort of doggerel:—

   Strike for the Anglo-Saxon!
    Strike for the newer day!
  O strike for heart and strike for brain,
    And sweep the *beast* away.

    And let no feeble pity
   Your sacred arms restrain;
  This is God's mighty moment
   To make an end of Spain!

It is our purpose to endeavour to make an end of the immoral inspiration behind this profane piffle by speaking out our mind on the subject of war as viewed from the standpoint of ethics.

By war we understand the appeal to *might* to decide a question of *right* between two or more civilised peoples, and of war thus defined I say that it is the great surviving infamy[1] of our unmoral past, the persistence in us of animal instincts, of the ape and tiger which should long since have died out. That man, in the childhood of the world, should have decided questions of justice by an appeal to brute force is only what we should expect. The laws of life, which are laws of development, necessarily presuppose the imperfect before the perfect, the animal as a preparation for the human. As

Immanuel Kant puts it in a sentence which flashes the light over the whole panorama of existence, "the *cosmic* evolution of Nature is continued in the *historic* development of humanity and completed in the *moral* perfection of the individual". This is the synthesis of the greatest of the masters of modern philosophy. The non-moral cosmos makes way for a process of moral human development, which is consummated in the perfection of each individual man. Here is the *Alpha* and *Omega* of all existence.

Now, warfare, or the invocation of might to settle right, was as natural an accompaniment of earlier conditions as theft or cannibalism. But is it not obvious that with the disappearance of other unmoral ideals of the past, we have a right to expect, and to demand, that the last and crowning infamy of wholesale and systematised manslaughter, called war, should cease also? The humanity which has got rid of slavery in all civilised countries, which has now through England's instrumentality succeeded in destroying its last strongholds on the Upper Nile, will also ultimately get rid of war. The manhood of the race, which in this country has long since put down the immorality of duelling as a means of settling private differences, will indubitably assert itself elsewhere to the final overthrow of warfare as a means of deciding public disputes. The great reform is in the air. It is everywhere except in the pulpits of Christendom and the "yellow press"—the jingo journalism of the world. We all experienced the growing sense of the unsuitability of war to our modern ideals during the earlier months of this year while matters were reaching the acute stage between Spain and the United States. The best Press in this country reflected the common sentiment, that the whole proceeding is savage, barbarous, inhuman, and therefore utterly unworthy of rational men. I believe it is this growing horror of legalised carnage which prevented the late President of the United States' ill-judged message leading to any rupture between our two countries. It was felt that Englishmen and Americans deliberately setting about the destruction of each other's property and taking one another's lives would amount to a scandal positively unthinkable—a fratricidal horror to be prevented at all and any costs. I am not sure that the same opinion was so universal on the other side, though undoubtedly it existed amongst the best men of the country.

America has at present two difficulties to contend with. First, she is a *young* nation, and young people are fond of trying experiments. And, next, they are burdened, perhaps I should say cursed, with the most violent, anti-cosmopolitan Press anywhere existent. A set of fire-eaters appear to control the New York section, of it, and in the judgment of many sober-minded Americans, with some of whom I have myself spoken, the late war was wholly due to their ceaseless, incessant clamour, and that, given a few months' patience, the Cuban people might have by plebiscite been able to settle their own destiny. The starving peasants concentrated in the towns were the alleged object of the hurry. Long months passed before any succour reached them. If they were veritably starving, surely every man of them must have died long before an American army of liberation could have been effectually landed for their relief. The sympathies of this country were not with Spain, for it is by her misrule, her acknowledged misgovernment of her colonists, that all the mischief has been brought about. One regrets to have to say it, but Spain has been strangled in the coils of her own superstition, and progress for her ceased to be when she elected to live by the light of ideals and principles which are henceforth impossible. It is the frantic endeavour of France and Italy to escape Spain's doom which explains their incessant strife between Church and State. The enlightened Frenchman or Italian has a horror of sacerdotalism as the beginning of the end, always and everywhere, and as the only religion in those countries is sacerdotal, they are, alas, in their national capacity, bereft of any religious guidance or inspiration. We are, therefore, unable to see anything in Spain's present position, but the working of the inevitable law of Compensation, which is sovereign over States as over individuals, though there are many of us who believe that the avowed humanitarian objects of the American Government might have been attained by peaceful methods, had not the country been goaded into a fever of restlessness and impatience by that deplorable phenomenon of democratic institutions known as the "yellow press".

At all events, the feeling universal in this country in the early spring of this year, showed how far and fast we are travelling along the road which will lead us to the final abandonment of warfare as unworthy of rational men. Doubtless we are in advance of other nations in this respect. But that is only what history leads us to expect. We were the first to free slaves, abandon duelling, reform prisons and criminal law, and erect humanitarianism into a veritable religion. And have we not taught representative institutions to the world? We are evidently destined, I believe, to lead the way towards the final surrender of war. We keep no standing army. We shall never again enter on a war of conquest or aggression. Our naval armaments and such military power as we possess are notoriously created and maintained for defensive purposes only. Brigandage and pillage we have most certainly been guilty of in past times, but such a policy could not now survive the day it was mooted. We are in the last trenches, preparatory to finally abandoning the field.

But here it will be urged that there are circumstances which render war absolutely inevitable, such for instance as an unjust aggression upon the territory we own, or even live upon; an attack on the national honour, or a reckless disregard of rights sanctioned by treaty or international usage. Were arbitration in such cases even admissible, we may conceive the would-be aggressor unwilling to have recourse to it, or possibly to abide by its award. What is a government to do then?

Now, arguments and pleas such as these are valid enough against a proposal of universal disarmament to be compulsorily carried out in six months or a year's time, but they in no wise, I submit, constitute an inseparable bar to the realisation of "that sweet dream," as Immanuel Kant called it, of a "perpetual peace". The ideal is none the less real because it cannot be at once put into practice; and had we to wait another whole century, it would still be the duty of our movement to stand by Kant and boldly set up the grand conception of an universal peace as the goal for which all that is best among men is inevitably making. Still, I trust that in our enthusiasm for ethic and for the ideal of its master, we have not lost our heads and betaken ourselves to Utopian impracticabilities. No ethical man could think of fixing a limit within which a national disarmament must take place, and the swords of the world beaten into ploughshares, any more than he could name the date at which the millennium is to be introduced. But this implies no insuperable, or rather, no serious, obstacle to our belief that the ideal of universal arbitration, through the medium of a congress of all nations, must in the future, near or distant, be realised, because it is an ideal which is alone worthy of rational men. And, moreover, the essential rationality of the ideal gives us a right to demand that it should be recognised by all public men, by our legislators who represent us, the Press which aims at reflecting the life and thought of the age, the professors and masters who have the care of our youth, and above all by fathers and mothers to whom tender children are confided, and those men who assume the responsibility of speaking to their generation in the sacred name of religion.

I say the ideal gives us the right to demand its recognition by men in such positions of responsibility, and implies a corresponding obligation on their part, no less than on our own, to labour seriously for its speedy realisation. We are, every one of us, agreed that war is essentially a cruel, barbarous, horribly vindictive and degrading method of serving the interests of the sublimest thing known to man, namely, justice. Wanton warfare, merely for the sake of fighting or killing, or openly avowed oppression, can scarcely be acknowledged now even by the most cynical of statesmen. The public conscience is become too sensitive for that, so that some question of justice, or the semblance of it, must be invoked in order to justify its unspeakable barbarities. But what an outrage, the deliberate destruction of hundreds of thousands of innocent men—men who in their simplicity or ignorance are positively unable to even dimly comprehend why they are being lashed into a blind fury and goaded to the madness of steeping their hands in each other's blood—what barbarity, what savagery to invoke as the minister, as the vindicator of justice! Let us keep our eyes steadily fixed on this central, essential wickedness of the whole business, that it dares to offer its polluted services in the interests of justice and thereby to profane the holiest thing we know.

Remembering this, therefore, let us ask ourselves what help we get in our endeavours to effect its overthrow from the recognised ministers of religion. Why, it is notorious that what has long been clear to philosophers like Immanuel Kant, and philanthropists among humble laymen, has not yet dawned upon the imagination or touched the consciences of bishops or priests. Popes, themselves, have created military orders, "knights and commanders of Christ and the Cross," whose profession it was to destroy life in the name of the most merciful, pitiful man known to us Western people. Popes have led military expeditions, conducted campaigns and crossed swords with the most daring, though the impetuous fisherman, founder of their line, was bidden by Christ to put up his sword into its scabbard, "for all they that take up the sword shall perish by it". Can any man point to one single condemnation of war as immoral, irrational, opposed to the law of their Deity or of Christ, in all the collection of councils, bulls and canonical legislation? And can any man quote to us the charge of an archbishop or bishop in the Anglican Communion or the Greek

Communion wherein he has raised his voice against the barbaric survival of war and condemned it in the name of his Saviour Jesus, who spoke of the meek, the mourners, the merciful, the pure in heart, the hungerers and thirsters after righteousness, or, as we say, the ethical enthusiasts, as his followers?

Why, religion, in the hands of bishops and priests, has allowed a trail of blood to be drawn across the path of the ages. I say nothing of religious persecution and the millions who have gone to torture and to doom for erroneous beliefs. I confine myself entirely, to field warfare. During a period of 674 years, from 1141-1815, it is an historical fact that this country and France were at war for no less than 266 years, or considerably more than one-third, and we must remember that up to the Reformation both countries were under the direct guidance, one might almost say the exclusive inspiration, of the Catholic Christianity of the day. But where does history record the act of any religious leaders of those times denouncing war as contrary to the gospel of Christ and of reason alike? We are able to quote numbers of despised heretics who had grasped the truth and emphatically condemned the brutal institution. Thus Erasmus: "They who defend war must defend the dispositions which lead to war, and these dispositions are absolutely forbidden by the gospel". Wickliffe, "the morning star of the Reformation in England," thought it "utterly unlawful," according to Priestley; and as Southey writes in his *History of Brazil*: "There is but one community of Christians in the world, and that unhappily of all communities one of the smallest, enlightened enough to understand the prohibition of war by the Divine Master in its plain literal and undeniable sense and conscientious enough to obey it, subduing the very instinct of nature to obedience".

These facts are noteworthy because they show that had the official churches—the Roman, Greek and Anglican—been true to their charge and commission from their founder; had they been unworldly enough to defy the world and denounce its barbarous practices, we might have been far nearer Kant's "sweet dream" of universal peace. But the churches, *as churches*, have done very little for the cause of the "Prince of peace," and now the world itself has outgrown their moral standard and looks to them for guidance and inspiration no more. By the light of reason alone, by the inspiration we gather from the *grands esprits* of the race, above all by the teaching of Immanuel Kant in his beautiful treatise on "Perpetual Peace," we intend to do what in us lies to put down this surviving, crowning infamy of war, the very thought of which brutalises the mind, outrages its humanitarian instincts, and degrades the ideals whereby we desire to live.

But, surely, it will be urged, we cannot refuse to acknowledge undoubted benefits, both public and individual, which war has conferred in the past. It has welded nomad peoples into nations, bred courage, devotion, loyalty, unselfishness, self-sacrifice even to death in the hearts of those who have nobly borne their part therein. Is not the soldier hero, the military chieftain, the idol of all mankind?

Doubtless he is, and unquestionably through the instrumentality of war great services have been rendered to the communities of peoples in the past and noble individual traits of character created. It is an axiom with us that the universe is so wondrously ordered that out of the worst things a soul of good may and does emerge, and so goodly is creation that its very evils become a source wherefrom good may arise.

What was good shall be good with for evil so much good more.

Thus, for example, the young lieutenant ordered to sink a hulk across the bay of Santiago, and his handful of companions have, by exposing themselves to imminent risk of an awful death, deeply stirred the feelings of their fellow-countrymen and filled us all with a sense of admiration at the heroism which can contemn danger and death in the execution of duty or the quest of glory. But we must ask whether humanity is in need of such exhibitions of bravery, whether there are not other fields of danger which offer tasks equally arduous and difficult of accomplishment? We are not insensible to the claims of military or naval heroism, but I confess I see much more to admire in Father Damien voluntarily surrendering himself to the slow and loathsome martyrdom of Molokai, more in the self-devotion of our "white slaves," as they must, alas! be called, who toil all the day and a deal of the night in a heavy, noisome, almost disease-laden atmosphere in the disgracefully crowded slums of our great cities, and all to earn a few pence wherewith to buy just enough bread to keep body and soul together in themselves and their children. Think of the matchbox-makers, who turn out a gross for a few halfpence, out of which they must supply some of their own materials. Think of the seamstresses, the shirt-makers and tailors' assistants in the veritable dens of East London, who by slaving for fifteen hours out of twenty-four can earn eighteenpence a day, out of which four or five shillings must be paid weekly for rent. Think of these mean, squalid surroundings in which a life of positively ceaseless toil must be lived, the patience and long-suffering with which it is endured, the silent martyrdom of monotonous, unrelieved existence prolonged over long years. Think of it, I say, and compare it with the intoxication of the battle-field, the cavalry charge, the roar of cannon and musketry, the rapid movements and counter-movements, the exultation which the sight of numberless men produces, grim, deadly determination on their faces, the thought of glory, the hope of renown, the dash of a few minutes, the stroke perhaps of a few seconds, the wild burst of untamed, savage human nature temporarily released from the restraint of reason! What cannot, what shall not man under such circumstances accomplish? Yes, we are not insensible to deeds of immortal daring, of courage, that must live for ever; nor to the memory of Leonidas and his Spartans, of the deathless glories of Thermopylae, of the unbroken chain of chivalric deeds from the days of ancient Greece to "the thin red line" that broke the fiercest charge, and the handful of Englishmen that shot away their last cartridge and then stood to die with their country's anthem on their lips—we are not insensible to all this, but we say the day for it is past and gone, and the heroism of the battle-field must be consecrated anew to the service of peace and the poor. The millions on millions we are spending on those majestic engines of destruction, those ships of ours that bastion the brine for England, what could they not do for the moralisation of the poor and outcast at our very doors in this city! Why, in three years that inferno of the East End, that foul, reeking, pestilential nest of tenements, unfit for even animal habitation, could be swept clean away and human homes erected which, to put it on the lowest grounds, would positively pay a dividend on the capital outlay, as has been convincingly proved over and over again.

"How long, O Lord, how long," we exclaim with the prophet of old, shall men be consumed with this ignoble fever, this war-madness which degrades the combatants far more than it exalts them, which senselessly destroys valuable property, scatters ruin broadcast, paralyses industry, robs the poor of all the bread of life, fills the land with mourning and desolation, with widows and orphans?—war, which we learnt from wild beasts, our ancestors, which cannot therefore determine a question of justice, which makes the wrong triumph as often as the right, which degrades all that touch it by isolating them for months, for years perhaps, from civilised life, which demoralises the victors, embitters the vanquished, and, by creating strife, perpetuates the possibilities of renewed strife—war, which at this moment keeps Europe in the condition of an armed camp, millions of men leading comparatively idle lives, with long hours on their hands which they cannot fill, with the inevitable results, the nauseating record of filth, disease and abominations too utterly loathsome even to think about—war, which is the curse of the poor and unfortunate, consuming the energies of men and the material means whereby their unhappy lot might be alleviated—war, the hard, cruel, relentless, inexorable monster of unregenerate man's creation—we, since no pope, bishop or priest will do it—we execrate it in the name of all we hold holiest, in the name of reason, morality and religion, and we pledge ourselves so to act, privately and politically, as to promote such measures—a federation of all English-speaking nations of the earth, if that will serve the purpose, or any other method equally or more serviceable—as will finally exorcise this last of the besetting demons of humanity, and fulfil thereby the "sweet dream" of our master and inspirer, Immanuel Kant.

    Ring out the old, ring in the new;
  * * * * *
Ring out the false, ring in the true;
Ring out old shapes of foul disease;
  Ring out the narrowing lust of gold;
  Ring out the thousand wars of old;
Ring in the thousand years of peace.

---

[1] Since these words were written the *Daily Chronicle* of 10th September, 1898, quotes them as having been used by a distinguished living English general.

XI.

THE ETHICS OF MARRIAGE.

There is probably no department of morality in which a metaphysic of ethic is more conspicuously needed than in that which concerns marriage. The insurrection of woman against the disabilities to which her sex was in the past unjustly subjected, due perhaps more to custom and tradition than to the statute law of the land, has developed in more recent times into a serious attack on the central institution of civilised life, on that fundamental fact of Nature on which posterity and society repose. We have had an outbreak in literature culminating in the giddy glory of the "hill-top novel," with its heroine "who did," and in America what is tautologically described as the "Free-Love Society" was founded to propagate the truth of what Rousseau euphemistically describes as *mariage après la nature*. For all that, however, one seems to hear less of the "hill-top" species, and possibly—with the problem play, without which no theatre was complete a couple of years ago—it may be fading into the mist of the past. It is with communities, we may take it, as with individuals. There are moments when, as it has been said, "every one is an atheist, from archbishops downwards," when a sense of the purposelessness and futility of perpetual combat seizes the most ardent. These are the dark hours when attacks are planned and delivered against the most sacred institutions, when people are not at their best, but are restless, rebellious and impatient of restraint; for nations like individuals can go mad. Then it is that the wide-awake novelist and playwright see their opportunity, and the temporary success of the sex-play or the breezy romance is the reflection of the thoughts—none of the best—that are for the moment flitting through men's feverish minds. But we soon return to saner moments; our moral sense resumes its normal sway, and sex-plays and romances fade away into oblivion.

Now, it need not be said that the contention on behalf of the rights of woman is heartily espoused by a movement which bases itself on the conception of reason and justice as the root facts of existence. There was no justice in the "subjection of woman," and we hold that those opportunities of learning which a cultured age opens up to man should likewise be at the disposal of his sister; that that freedom, which is the birthright of the man, to expand the energies, mental and moral, of his being to their fullest extent and in whatever calling, should also be acknowledged to be the right of woman. The constitutional agitation for the recognition of her rights has met with notable success, and it has the fullest support of the ethical Church; but we believe that that agitation has been pushed too far by a very small and insignificant minority, and made to cover an attack on the institution of matrimony, which her wisest friends see could only end in the ultimate downfall of woman herself. Such an agitation, such an attack, must encounter the most resolute opposition from a body which derives all its idealism and inspiration from a life motived, not by the sense, but by reason. Its leaders in America have pronounced decisively against any tampering with the natural sacrament of marriage, and where they detect tendencies—as unfortunately they do in many of the States of their Union—to further loosen its bonds, they, with all the influence at their command, endeavour to strengthen them.

Let me now proceed to justify this attitude of the ethical communion.

We do not base our action on considerations of authority such as move the Churches of Christendom. It is not because Jesus assisted at a wedding breakfast and performed an alleged wonder; not because the Apostle Paul calls marriage "a great mystery in Christ and the Church," but because both Jesus and Paul and the Churches express a truth of nature itself, that the union of man and woman is not, and cannot be, the herding of animals; that the bestowal of the body cannot but be the outward symbol of an invisible bond which is the very soul and life of the contract. We thus go behind all Churches and apostles and ascend to the very roots of Nature herself, and discern in the golden glory wherewith she surrounds the ideal marriage the significance of her intentions in its regard—that it is her true and real Sacrament, that her sons and daughters are themselves its ministers, for they alone are kindled with the heavenly fire; that not the Church, not the priest nor ritual celebrates it, but these twain made one by that same

Love which moves the earth and heavens and all the stars.

That man has so regarded marriage as a sacred and sacramental fact is authenticated by history in an abundantly available form. No doubt, ages must have passed before he emerged from his animalesque condition and abandoned polygynous and polygamous manners, the marriage by capture and purchase, which were the stages which mark the historical evolution of the contract. But ultimately these barbaric stages passed away, and we discover in the Teutonic ancestors of Britain that monogamy which was Nature's ideal from the first. Just as man was potential in the primordial slime, so was the marriage of Robert Browning a possibility in the earliest union of scarce-emancipated man and woman. What the institution *could* become, what it *has* become, shows what was the intent of Nature from the beginning. In the nobler days of Rome, under the republic and early empire, the same lofty conception animated her best sons. It was the decay of reverence for the sacred bond, the era when a woman's years were told by the number of her divorces, which called forth the solemn warnings of her moralist poets and philosophers, and ultimately brought about the emasculation of the nation's manhood and the downfall of the empire. We have not the remotest doubt but that a similar contempt in modern Europe for Nature's ordinance would involve us in the same catastrophe. A low estimate of marriage means contempt of woman; the contempt of woman means her degradation from her position at the side of man as his counsellor and his friend to that of his plaything, the instrument of his pleasure; that again means the enthronement of licence and licentiousness; that, the softening of the brain power of the manhood of the race, leading to degeneracy, imbecility, and ultimate extinction. We need no ecclesiastical organisation to tell us these things, nor threaten us with direst penalties here or hereafter. These are the penalties of nature's own aboriginal enactment. As it was in the beginning, so it is now, and so it shall be unto all time. No wonder St. Paul called marriage "a great mystery"!

Now, though it be true that Nature's ideal is that which we call monogamy, it may be perfectly true that we have not yet reached that level of morality which makes that condition universally practicable. That wisest of teachers, Jesus of Nazara, expressly recognised this distinction when he told the Jews of his own day that their lack of ethical enthusiasm, "their hardness of heart," as he accurately expressed it, the emptiness of their souls of everything save narrow nationalism and religious formalism—an emptiness by no means peculiar to them—was the sole reason which justified a departure from Nature's great ideal. "In the beginning it was not so," he declared, but "Moses gave ye permission to write out a bill of divorce". That one exception may be necessary still, but, let it be understood, it is not the ideal, and every one knows it, faithful and faithless alike, they whose honour is intact and they whose souls are smirched. It is an instinct in the human heart—no one can deny it—that love is for evermore. Shakespeare is right, "Marriage is a world-without-end bargain," for love is felt to be eternal. The old Roman digest interprets nature with philosophic accuracy when it describes marriage as "*Conjunctio maris et feminae et consortium omnis vitae, divini et humani juris communicatio*". "The union of man and woman and the companionship of all life, the sharing of right, human and divine." That is the majestic conception of matrimony as it took shape in the brain of those Roman masters of jurisprudence to whom we owe the law which is the nerve of civilisation. They learnt it from that ethical religion which we, too, reverently follow, from that morality which they found *in things, in themselves*, in Nature's plain teaching that the union of man and his wife was a sacramental fact and therefore indelible.

Are we asked for further evidence of this position? We see it as a law of our rational being, which refuses to believe that Nature makes no other provision for us than she does for the animals; that their instinctive and impulsive association should be the norm of man's intercourse with woman. Nay, we see Nature herself as she advances to the higher stages of animal existence anticipating, in a sense, that ideal which was only to be fully realised in man. The lion, the king of beasts, as he is called, tends towards that ideal, and the elephant is believed to be even more strictly monogamous. The loves of birds, of doves and pigeons, are too well known to need more than a passing mention, and the grief they experience on the death of their partner not unfrequently ends in a broken heart. But how much better is man than many animals, and what is merely instinctive in them shall not he consciously obey as his acknowledged law of life?

We may see the truth also in Nature's ordinance, that man's offspring must be educated in order to reach maturity; that training of a serious character is indispensably necessary to the development of the powers latent in them. But how is such training possible, except through the unceasing watchfulness of the parents'? People here and there darken counsel with the suggestion that the State should assume such responsibilities. Was there ever such a suggestion? As a matter of mere finance, we are told by the Vice-President of the Council, that the assumption of the quite partial responsibility for the education of the children now taught in the elementary schools of the denominational bodies of the country, would mean an addition of some millions yearly to the rates. The education rate is high enough in all conscience, but where the "hill-top" theory would land us one can scarcely conjecture. So urgent is this consideration of the claim which offspring has upon parent, so imperative the need that children should be fittingly instructed so as to be worthy citizens of a great community, that we find writers like Karl Pearson, in his *Ethic of Free Thought*,[1] consistently excepting from the operation of the free-love gospel those unions which have resulted in the procreation of children. Mr. Pearson being of the school of those who deride marriage as "the tomb of love," "the source of the stupidity and ugliness of the human race," his admissions as to the necessity of maintaining some element of permanence in the contract, if only for the sake of children, is well worthy of our attention. It shows how grounded in nature is that conception of the marriage tie which the Roman digest has put before us.

We may see the truth, once again, in the acknowledged instability of the passional element in human nature—particularly in man. It is nothing short of amazing to see this very instability urged as a reason why the marriage tie should be still further weakened, as though man should deliberately subject himself to the vagaries of sense, instead of the guidance of reason. We hear much to-day about the "return to nature," and, soundly interpreted, that gospel sounds like a breath of pure mountain air after the stifling atmosphere of modern convention and unreality. Would to heaven, I say from my heart, that we were more natural, that a greater frankness and directness marked our intercourse with one another, that the shams and pretences of so much of our social life were made away with, that our lives were more open and free! The grand old Stoic maxim had it thus: *Live in accordance with nature.* Yes, but with what nature? No thinker, from Socrates to Kant, from Buddha to Hegel, ever had a doubt but that man's nature was twofold, and that the law of reason must be supreme in him. Let an animal live for sense; it is its nature; but for man another law is ordained, which bids him think last of enjoyment, and to partake only of that in obedience to the law of the mind. The modern evangel of the apotheosis of the unstable we understand to convey the teaching, "Live in accordance with sense, or the feeling of the moment". Be like the *dame du monde* whom Mrs. Ward has so accurately drawn in *Madame de Netteville*, who did not hold herself responsible to our petty codes, and judged that feeling was guidance enough for her. That may be all very well for Madame de Netteville, but how does such teaching look in the light of Kant's solemn injunction: "Act so that thy conduct may become a law unto all men"? Could any one seriously propose to erect feeling into a supreme criterion whereby to judge of the conduct of life?

And, to show that the line of argument here adopted is no mere false asceticism surviving from an undisciplined and pre-scientific age, as the solemn verbiage of so much second-rate talking expresses it to-day, we may quote some words of David Hume, Huxley's "prince of agnostics," from the *Essay on Polygamy and Divorce*. The least emotional of philosophers—a hard-headed Scotsman—he makes short work of the sentimentality which is invoked now-a-days against the natural law of marriage:—

"We need not be afraid of drawing the marriage knot . . . the closest possible. The unity between the persons, where it is solid and sincere, will rather gain by it; and where it is wavering and uncertain that is the best method for fixing it. How many frivolous quarrels and disgusts are there, which people of common prudence endeavour to forget, when they lie under the necessity of passing their lives together; but which would soon be inflamed into the most deadly hatred, were they pursued to the utmost under the prospect of an easy separation! We must consider that nothing is more dangerous than to unite two persons so closely in all their interests and concerns, as man and wife, without rendering the union entire and total. The least possibility of a separate interest must be the source of endless quarrels and suspicions. The wife, not secure of her establishment, will still be driving some separate end or project; and the husband's selfishness, being accompanied by no power, may be still more dangerous." Thus our conception of marriage as a nature sacrament, a permanent contract in Nature's original intention, is abundantly confirmed by the sceptical philosopher of the eighteenth century. Whatever man may make of the contract, there stands the fact that that Nature meant it to be enduring which whispered into the lover's heart that "love should be for evermore".

It is a far cry from the abstractions of philosophy to the realisms of French fiction, but we could not better conclude this portion of our subject than by citing one single sentence from Balzac, in the judgment of many the first romancer of this century, and one of the greatest masters of the social sciences. "Nothing," he declares, "more conclusively proves the necessity of indissoluble marriage than the instability of passion."

But here our difficulties begin. Though it may be abundantly clear that Nature's ideal is Hume's and Balzac's, is it not a fact that this "high has proved too high, this heroic for earth too hard"? Is it not true that there are murmurs and mutterings of revolt both amongst men and women against a burden too grievous to be borne? Does not the fiction of the day represent a tendency to allow an increased laxity in the interpretation of the matrimonial contract? And where there is smoke there is fire. What novelists write other people are thinking. Has the time come to reconsider our position with regard to marriage and the permanent obligations hitherto associated with it?

We answer decisively, No. It is not the institution which is at fault, but the individuals who embrace it. We spoke of marriage as Nature's great sacrament, and so it is. And as with "the Lord's Supper" the unworthy participant is said to "eat and drink only condemnation to himself," so is it with they who draw near to Nature's banquet and attempt, unprepared, to partake of the deepest joys of life. Their profanity smites them with a curse. We hold up our hands in no Pharisaic spirit of holy horror, but we ask the men and women of this generation and of those classes from which these mutterings and threatenings of revolt mainly emanate—we ask them, whether marriage, as they understand the term, can be other than a bloodless martyrdom? If that individual who gave her name to a novel two or three seasons ago, if the young woman known as *Dodo* be a type—and it was noted by the critics of the time that such was the character of the fashionable young *mondaine* of the day, greedy for nothing but excitement and sensuous existence, incapable of serious thought, rebellious against, I will not say the restraints, but even the *convenances* of civilised life, with no pretension to anything remotely resembling character or moral earnestness, a wild, gay, frittering, helpless creature, whom it were blasphemy to think of in the same day with noble womanhood as we all have known it—if *that*, I say, is the type of the young *mondaine* of the hour, then I have no doubt they will give the novelists and playwrights plenty of employment in describing their self-imposed torments, the insufferable bondage to which they are subjected. But does any one propose to alter the moral law for them? If mothers in modern Babylon are ready to labour day and night in attempting to catch as husbands for their daughters men in whom one and one only qualification is asked, namely, that of wealth, then their perdition be upon their own heads and on those of the luckless pair who are literally speaking "crucified on a cross of gold". If girls continue to be brought up with the preposterous notion that marriage is the one profession open to them, and that therefore they are by no means to risk the loss of an "engagement," no matter who the employer may be, and that the wealthier he is the more suitable he is to be adjudged, then let us abandon all attempts at reaching our ideal. But let us at the same time prepare for the overthrow of the home and the family; for the destruction of "pure religion breathing household laws," and of the stately, dignified, domestic life, which has been the glory of every land where Nature's true ideal has been worthily upheld.

If boys are brought up at school, or taught by the social atmosphere they breathe on first entering into early manhood, to conceive of marriage as in no wise nobler or loftier in essence than any of those *mariages après la nature*, those ephemeral associations, terminable at will; that the only difference between them is, that the one is legal and permanent, the other voluntary and dissoluble, then so long will the scandals of divorce and the revolt against marriage continue to be heard. What one complains of is the utter lack of reverence in the view which is taken of this most solemn of all acts. There is no idealism in the contract. The thoughtless youth who has grown up in what one may call the "wild oats" theory is, we suggest, utterly incapable of appreciating the absolutely inestimable blessings which wedded love might have brought him. How can he? He has "wasted his substance, living riotously," and the most precious of all the treasures he has squandered is that of his idealism. *His wife can scarcely be to him what she might have been had he come to her as he expected her to come to him.* "The golden gates are closed," "a glory has passed from the earth". This is pain enough to make hearts weep, but it is the operation of that inflexible law of Compensation, that not all the tears of sorrow, not all the absolutions and sacrificial atonements of Churches, can undo that past, can make that young man to be as in the days of his youth, before the experimental "knowledge of good and evil" touched him.

Our remedy is, therefore, not to destroy the institution of Nature, but to reform the candidates who undertake to embrace it. An ethical religion would reprobate the sacrilegious bargains in which bodies are exchanged for gold, and refuse to accord them the honorific title of marriage, which is first and foremost a union of souls. Time and again have we seen that the springs of all things are in the invisible world, from the breath of a flower to the energy that pulsates in the great bosom of the ocean, or governs the movements of the uttermost star. It is so here. Not the transference of bodies, of titles, of wealth or station, are the sacrament. They are merely the accessories, the outward form, the symbol of something higher and Diviner far, of the invisible love, which is everywhere, yet manifests itself in especial manner in these two souls, speaking even in their very countenances of an emotion supreme and irresistible. An ethical religion, wholly based upon and identified with morality, would refuse to sanction any marriage but that we have described, a union based upon a supreme affection between two who had worthily prepared themselves for its consummation, and believed in the permanence of their tie.

With regard to the modern maiden—the *Dodos* and their kindred swains—it would be infinitely preferable that they did not degrade the sanctity of a natural sacrament by profanely prostituting it to their temporal and social convenience. Far better that they betook themselves to "the marriage after the truth of nature" than to the great human institution of which Milton sang:—

Hail, wedded love, mysterious law,
True source of human offspring!

They do but defile it by their patronage, and having manifestly spoiled themselves by their reckless lives for the entertainment of any emotion deeper than mere sensuousness, they are bound at length to bring a noble institution into contempt, and drag it down in their own fall. You do not believe, we would say to them, in the eternity of soul and love, and therefore the nature sacrament is not for you. But having presented yourselves at its sacred table, and partaken of its rites, do not, if only for motives of mere decency, betake yourselves to the denunciation of that of which, indeed, you were never worthy.

Week by week, at the services of the ethical Church, we see numbers of young men who doubtless aspire one day to share in the benediction which a true marriage alone can bring them. Their presence is welcome as a testimony to the virility and inspiration of the ethic creed which is strong enough to prevail over other inducements which would take them far afield. It shows that spirit overcomes the flesh, and that the culture of the mind is not postponed to the relaxation and enjoyment of the body.

What the ethical religion says to all such as they is this: Live so as to be worthy of that which you one day hope to receive at Nature's hands—a pure, good and true wife. Somewhere, in some corner of this earth, unknown to you, unknown to her, she is being made ready for the hour of your espousals. You will know her when you see her. Wait until you do. Remember the requisite preparation of the body, and now forget not the preparation of the mind.

Marriage is based on friendship, that true kinsman of love, which made a poet call his friend "O thou half of my own soul!" [2] Your wife must be your friend. True love, the love of which true marriages are made, is friendship transfigured—the halo, the glory, of a supreme emotion coming to crown that which is most enduring on this earth. Just as we say that our religion is morality, is duty, only etherealised by viewing it as the expressed mind and will of the Soul of all souls, the World-intelligence, so do we think of marriage as based on a union of souls by friendship, inspired by a deep mutual respect, not for what the partners have, but for what they are, and finally made glorious in the light of an unfading love. Live, we would counsel you, so as to be worthy one day of the reverence of a woman's pure and untried soul.

And our message to womanhood is not dissimilar. Live, we would say, so that you be worthy of the respect, of the homage of all men. Your nature is such that virtue in you has a double charm, wherefore you are visibly marked out as the treasury wherein the ideal is enshrined and handed down through all the generations of men.

A nation is, ethically speaking, worth just what its women are worth, and we must therefore rejoice, and greatly rejoice, to know that the contention which is being increasingly put forth by women, that the men who demand their sisters' hands should themselves be arrayed in suitable wedding garment, is convincing evidence of a strong ethical enthusiasm which is beginning to pervade the sex, and a determination to ennoble more and more that one great sacramental ordinance of Nature, marriage.

    All things transitory
 But as symbols are sent;
 Earth's insufficiency grows to event;
 The indescribable,
 Here it is done,
 The ever-womanly leadeth us
 Upward and on.
    —GOETHE.

[1] Pp. 431-443.

[2] "Dimidium animae meae" (Horace).

XII.

THE ETHICAL CHURCH AND POSITIVISM.

The appearance within the last hundred years of different philosophical attempts to produce a synthesis which should combine at once a system of thought for the guidance of the mind, and a source of enthusiasm for the inspiration of the heart, is significant of many things, but chiefly of two. In the first place it is evidence that the present has outgrown the past; that the religion of medievalism is inadequate to modern needs; that

> Still the new transcends the old,
> In signs and tokens manifold.

And, next, it would appear to indicate the serious disposition of the new Age. If we find the thinkers of humanity uniformly tending towards a given direction, we may be sure there is an undefined, perhaps unconscious, though none the less real, desire on the part of the age to be led thither. Thus, at the close of the last century, Immanuel Kant, while undermining the ground on which the faith of old rested, attempted that new presentation of religion, as essential and sovereign morality, with which we are so familiar. And, within half a century of the foundation of the new Church, we meet with another bold and comprehensive effort to revivify religion, which had grown cold in the heart of his country, by showing that its chief expression is to be found in that "love of the brotherhood" whereby Jesus

Christ declared his own truest followers would ever be known. "We tire of thinking and even of acting," this foremost of the thinkers of his age declared, but "we never tire of loving". I need not say that these are the words of Auguste Comte, one of the two men in this nineteenth century who had learning enough to grasp the universal knowable, and genius enough to express it in a clearly defined philosophic system. His fellow and compeer, of course, is our own Herbert Spencer.

Now, no one will be able to even dimly appreciate the significance of the work of Immanuel Kant and Auguste Comte unless he realises that the inspiration which moved them both was that which we call religion. As the rivers flow into the sea, so the streams of knowledge converge at a point which marks the limits of the finite, the boundaries of the Infinite. There never was a system of thought yet which did not culminate in the sublimity of religion. From the first system of all, the immortal Aristotle's, down to Kant's, Comte's and Spencer's in our own times, the issue is always the same: philosophy leads the way to the Boundless; it lifts the veils of the Eternal. And therefore Kant and Comte, each in his own way, while setting forth their exposition of intellectual truth, endeavoured to provide a stimulus to move the heart of man to put its plain teachings into execution.

Though at first sight there appears to be nothing but irreconcilable opposition between the critical and positivist systems, there is, nevertheless, a fundamental unity which Comte was quick enough to detect, for he pronounced Kant "the most positive of all metaphysicians". What led him to this conviction was the fact that the German philosopher had, like himself, based his whole idealism on the sure ground of morality which cannot be overthrown. As Spinoza was called by Novalis "a God-intoxicated man," so Comte was described by Mill as "morality-intoxicated," for in the purity and elevation of his ethical conceptions he comes nearest of all to the austere standard set up by Kant and Emerson.

Nor do the points of resemblance stop here. In the course of this chapter it will become ever more evident that there is no irreconcilable opposition between the ethical religion of Kant and the Religion of Humanity of Comte, nay, that there appears to be a well-grounded hope that the Church of the Future, which we salute from afar, and towards the building of which we are each contributing our share, will in the main embrace as its essential features the teaching of these two great men. For that Church will aspire to guide men in their private and in their public capacities, in their individual and in their social life. The ethic of Kant, the categorical imperative of duty, will be the inspiration of the individual; the *Politique Positive* of Comte will govern him in his social and political relations, while in the supreme concern of worship, I venture to foretell a widening of the Comtist ideal so as to admit of such conceptions as underlie the philosophical belief of Mr. Spencer, that the world and man are but "the fugitive product of a Power without beginning or end," whose essence is ineffable. Thus the agnosticism of to-day will contribute to the reverence of the future, while I firmly believe that the religion of Humanity will come to be so interpreted as not to wholly exclude belief in an Existence anterior to man and to all things, from whom he and all he knows aboriginally sprang, unto whom he and all things ultimately return. Nothing shall be lost of these words of life which have fallen from Wisdom's lips; they are treasured now in many hearts, and some day, near or distant, they will be one and all incorporated in some diviner gospel than any which has yet been heard, and preached in some church, vast enough, catholic enough, for the inspiration of the race. *Reposita est haec spes in sinu meo.*

In the meantime, we must attempt something of a succinct statement of the ethical, social and religious system with which the name of Auguste Comte is associated.

It is clear that he was early impelled to a study of the principles on which society rests by the disorganisation into which his country had fallen, after the upheaval of the Revolution and the disasters of the Napoleonic era which succeeded it. It may even be the truth that his bold and subversive teaching in religious matters was due to a profound conviction that the virtue of the old ideals had been completely exhausted, and that if society was to be regenerated, it must be by a radical reformation of the theoretic conceptions on which it had been held to repose. Certainly there was a vast deal in the contemporary history of France to confirm Comte in his belief that Catholicism had spent its force. At a period of crisis in a nation's history, thinking men naturally look about them for some strong influence, for some commanding ideal which can serve as a rallying point in times of social dispersion, and help to keep the severing elements of the body politic together. But what had religion done for France in the hour of her trial? So little, that the country had to wade through blood in order to reach a measure of political emancipation which England had long enjoyed. In fact, it was the corruption of religion in the person of its official representatives, its intellectual degradation in the eyes of the thinkers, which helped to provoke the catastrophe. What wonder, then, that a mind so penetrating and alert as Comte's early arrived at the conclusion that the *ancien régime* in religion, no less than in politics, must be abolished if progress was to be possible among men?

Comte, then, was essentially a social philosopher. His work, indeed, is encyclopaedic—not one whit less so than Spencer's—but the aim he persistently kept in view was the service of man by the reconstruction, through philosophy and religion, of the foundations on which civilisation rests. It is impossible not to be impressed by the grandeur of his conception, and the consuming energy with which he addressed himself to its realisation. He seems to recall to us Browning's Paracelsus, whose "vast longings" urged him forward to some surpassing achievement, to some heroic attempt

>To save mankind,
>To make some unexampled sacrifice
>In their behalf, to wring some wonderous good
>From heaven or earth for them.

When a young man of only twenty-four years, he had already published his first work, entitled *A Plan of Scientific Works necessary to reorganise Society*, thus striking the keynote of his career. We can feel nothing but the strongest admiration for the man who from the first determines to subordinate knowledge, life and love, to the service of the human race. It was Comte's incessant teaching that the sciences were to be cultivated, not as ends in themselves, but as means whereby to further human welfare. He would have the astronomer and physiologist pursue their tasks, not merely for the sake of acquiring knowledge, for the gratification of the curiosity to know, but for the betterment of man's lot. And for the same reason he insisted on the pre-eminence of the sympathetic affections over the intellect. The reason, he declared, must ever be the servant, *though not the slave*, of the emotions. Altruism, or the service of others (a word of his own coining), must be made to prevail over egoism or selfishness. There could not be a nobler conception of human duty.

What was the source of the miseries which had driven the people of France to rebellion but the selfishness of absolute monarchs, of dissolute nobles who ground their dependants to the dust of destitution, and of a corrupt hierarchy of clergymen contemptuous of the people, hypocritical in their conduct, and slaves of the crown? An astounding revelation that elementary religion should be preached again in France by a layman who had turned his back in disappointment on all that priests and the past represented!

And what is the source of the degradation of our own cities but this same curse of selfishness which is ready to march to opulence and luxury over the bodies of the starved and poisoned toilers of our towns and factories, and thinks it can justify its barbarity by an off-hand reference to Political Economy and its irrefragable laws? "Supply and demand"—sacrosanct enactments of man's brains—how shall they prevail over the clear dictates of the conscience that thunder in our ears that it is murderous to grind the life out of the poor in the name of an economical fetish? Is not the man more than the meat, and the body more than the raiment? How shall not man, then, be better than many economical laws? If the laws outrage our sense of justice, then are they false laws, because false to reason, and they must be abolished. The unrestricted domination of the competition theory which urges men to buy in the cheapest and sell in the dearest market, and pay the very lowest wages that poor outcasts are forced in their destitution to accept—is that to be the permanent condition of large masses of toilers in the towns of the richest country in the world? Is the matchbox-maker to go on for ever turning out a gross for 2 1/4d., providing her own paste and string? Are wretched women to toil from morning till night folding sheets—sheets of cheap bibles at 10s. a week and pay lodging and keep a family out of it? Are men and women to be decimated by consumption in the poisoned atmosphere of some of our factories? No commonwealth can exist on such a basis, and if economical laws are invoked in its support, those laws are an infamy. No wonder Carlyle fiercely denounced it all as "a wretched, unsympathetic, scraggy atheism and egoism".

Well, Auguste Comte had witnessed all this and possibly worse than this in France. He knew the institutions of his country and of his age, and he came to the deliberate conclusion that if any progress was to be made, if this degrading egoism was to be put down, this callous insensibility on the part of employers towards the labourers, whose slow martyrdom produces the wealth they enjoy, the whole scheme of social philosophy would have to be reconsidered and a new foundation provided whereon to build the commonwealth. "You want altruism in place of egoism; sympathy instead of selfishness," he preached. "How are you going to obtain it? For eighteen centuries now you have been walking in one beaten path, following one and the same light, listening to the same spiritual guides. What have they taught you? Whither have they led you? To the impasse which you have now reached. Has not the time come to begin anew; to reconstruct, to reorganise society? And this time it must be *sans dieu, sans roi, par le culte systématique de l'Humanité.*"

Such is the remedy proposed by Auguste Comte for the malady of the modern world; this is his revolutionary scheme for the establishment of society on such a basis as would conduce to progress. It involves, as may be seen, the disavowal of the belief in God and king; the substitution of a republic for a monarchy, and of humanity for God. Comte conceived religion as the concentration of the three great altruistic affections, namely, of *reverence* towards that which is above us; of *love* towards that which helps and sustains us, and *benevolence* towards that which needs our co-operation. Religion being in his judgment a supreme concern of life, though always subordinated to the larger interest of social welfare, he was anxious to provide the new commonwealth with an idealism which should set before man a Being able to evoke these three great emotions. Formerly man had bestowed them on God; Comte thought he had found a more excellent way in suggesting that they might far more appropriately and profitably be exercised on mankind. The service of God, therefore, being changed into the service of man, he contended that the course of things would set steadily in a higher direction, because all the immense energy and enthusiasm which the worship of God had been able to provoke in the past would be available in the cause of suffering, down-trodden and persecuted humanity. He wished to dam the stream of devotion flowing towards the churches and God, and divert it into channels that had far greater need of it—the unsatisfied and unprovided needs of all mankind.

Is it urged that religion apart from a belief in God is an impossibility? Doubtless such is the conviction of great numbers of people, and, it must be confessed, such usage of the word is not consonant with prevalent custom. Still the emotion which Comte experienced for Humanity was such as no other word would adequately express. As Mr. Mill remarks in his chapters on the Positivist System (p. 133)—

It has been said that whoever believes in the infinite nature of duty, even if he believe in nothing else, is religious. Comte believes in what is meant by the infinite nature of duty, but he refers the obligations of duty, as well as all sentiments of devotion, to a concrete object, at once ideal and real; the human race, conceived as a continuous whole, including the past, the present and the future. . . . Candid persons of all creeds may be willing to admit that if a person has an ideal object, his attachment and sense of duty towards which are able to control and discipline all his other sentiments and propensities, and prescribe to him a rule of life, that person has a religion. . . . The power which may be acquired over the mind by the idea of the general interest of the human race, both as a source of emotion and as a motive to conduct, many have perceived; but we know not if any one before Comte realised so fully as he has done all the majesty of which that idea is susceptible. It ascends into the unknown recesses of the past, embraces the manifold present, and descends into the indefinite and unforeseeable future.

Such is the famous *Law of the three States*, which has always been treated by friend and foe as the key to the Comtean philosophy. It only concerns us now to describe the use he made of it in abolishing the belief in God, and thus attempting to revolutionise the conception of religion.

Closely associated with his Law of the three States is another which he calls the *Law of the Wills and Causes*. In fact, there is practically no difference between that law and the first or theological stage through which human knowledge goes. It may be enunciated thus: Whenever the human mind is in ignorance of the proximate causes of a given phenomenon, it tends to ascribe it to the agency of superior and invisible powers. Hence, ignorance of nature, which modern science has largely remedied, led men to ascribe to "the act of God" innumerable events, even the appearance of Halley's comet, which we now unhesitatingly refer to subordinate agencies. Why, then, urged Comte, should we continue to believe in even one supreme Cause, when we may hope, with the advance of science, to give an explanation of every natural occurrence or fact? Convinced on social grounds that belief in the Deity had been of no service to mankind, he sought for philosophical reasons to justify his surrendering the tenet, and thus formulated the famous law which has just been enunciated. If that law is valid and universal in its application, we should have to surrender all hope of Comte's co-operation with what we hold to be rational religion. But it is because I am so convinced that it is that very law, so finely framed and stated by Comte, which makes it impossible to dispense with belief in a supra-mundane Power, that I adhere to the ideal which I sketched in the beginning, that Kant and Comte will be found to be, after Christ, the master builders of the second temple which is to be the religious home of the ages to come.

For what does his famous law amount to? To nothing beyond this, that we are warranted in believing that no single fact, no individual phenomenon, of nature exists, but will be one day explained by the all-conquering advance of physical science. But surely his most enthusiastic adherent will admit that when every phenomenon has been singly explained, only half the work, and that by far the less significant part, has been done. If the human mind is eager, and legitimately eager, to explore the scene of nature's manifestations, much more will it be necessary to attempt some solution of the vaster fact of their concatenation, of their miraculous combination into that whole which we call the universe. It is not so much the isolated phenomena which strike the mind with such overpowering bewilderment, as the manifest fact that in their infinite diversity and innumerable varieties, they are all subordinated to one vast end—the constitution and the good of the whole. Explain every sun that lines the eternal path into the Infinities, where no telescope can penetrate—what is that to the mind that knows that the numberless series is bound together by laws which they as unhesitatingly obey as an animal when it walks? Hence, by the very terms of his own law, Comte is compelled to restore to the human mind its belief in a Power other than the world, for if our only justification for discarding that belief is that science will explain one day the *individual* phenomena of the universe, it is plain that man's science can never hope to explain the origin of the worlds themselves and the infinite complexities of their mutual relations. And if science cannot hope to do that, the mind of man must, under penalty of going to disruption, assent to the belief that there is a World-Power who is responsible for the conscious production of the universe, and therefore of ourselves.

And I am glad to be able to say that Comte never expressly excluded this belief. On the contrary, he asserts that if a cosmic hypothesis is to be held at all, that of an intelligent Mind is far more probable than atheism. Indeed of atheism he has written as caustically as the most orthodox could wish. He expressly contends that the theory of design is far more probable than blind mechanism, and if he excludes theism, it is not so much for philosophical as for social reasons. Consumed with a passion for human betterment, seeing that the "love of God" had deplorably failed as an incentive to morality, he made the tremendous effort of endeavouring to substitute the love of man as a stimulus towards the accomplishment of duty. If Comte denied God, let the Churches and ecclesiastics of France and of Europe bear the responsibility. It was the disastrous condition into which Europe had fallen under their guidance which led him to despair of "God" as a rallying point for humanity.

But there is, I submit, no inherent necessity in the Positivist system to insist on the dogmatic exclusion of such theism as we profess under the guidance of Emerson and Kant, and it is gratifying to be able to quote so sympathetic a supporter as J. S. Mill in favour of this interpretation. "Whoever regards all events as parts of a constant order, each one being the invariable consequent of some antecedent condition, or combination of conditions, accepts fully the positivist mode of thought: whether he acknowledges or not an universal antecedent on which the whole system of nature was originally consequent, and whether that universal antecedent is conceived as an intelligence or not." [1]

I need not say that to us who believe in Mind as the necessary antecedent to all things, the positivist spirit, so defined, is essential truth. We believe in the Great Being revealed in the eternal order of the physical worlds and in the eternal order of the moral law. Our worship of God is therefore a worship of goodness or morality, an ideal of justice, as seen in the lives of only the elect spirits of the race, and thus "the worship of Humanity" is also the worship of God. For where is God revealed as *worshipful* except in the lives of the great and good? And if religion be defined to be morality as taught in the lives of the holiest servants of mankind, in what do we differ essentially from the ennobling conceptions of Auguste Comte? The service of man is seen to be the service of God, for we know nothing of God until we have learnt to serve goodness and minister to our brother man. The day will come when Comte will be honoured in the universal Church as an apostle of true religion, because, like Kant, he showed men that there is nothing holier or diviner on this earth than a life consciously conformed to the obedience of august laws. Comte, no less than his brother philosopher, is a servant of humanity, and therefore a servant of God, and we conceive that both thinkers have laid mankind under an immeasurable debt by showing us that that emotion of reverence which all men instinctively feel towards a Power greater than man, cannot be worthily satisfied except by a conscious endeavour to live as befits our rational nature, and to serve "the brethren" out of love.

[1] *Auguste Comte and Positivism*, p. 15.

XIII.

THE OLD FAITH AND THE NEW

AS SEEN IN *HELBECK OF BANNISDALE*.

Cynical observers of the tendencies of the age tell us that, like the Athenians of Paul's days, we are "lovers of new things". Doubtless we are, for this century, this "wonderful century," as it has recently been described, is a new age or there never was one. Hence, just as Spinoza saw everything *sub specie aeternitatis*, we may very well have a tendency to see many things *sub specie novi*. New things, astonishingly new things, in every imaginable department of life have been witnessed by men who saw the opening years of the century, and *fin-de-siècle* as we are, the capacities of man are apparently as inexhaustible as ever.

It would indeed be passing strange were religion an exception to the uniform progress everywhere in operation. Doubtless the aspect of that supreme concern of life does change less rapidly, but change it does and must: *eppur si muove*. And it is significant, as one of the most striking results of the beneficent movements of our time, that, in the English-speaking countries at least, one of the most powerful, because the most far-reaching, stimuli to religious progress has been supplied by the hand of a woman.

It has always seemed to me that Mrs. Humphry Ward's *Robert Elsmere* was the making of an epoch, and when so shrewd an observer of the times, so enthusiastic an admirer of "the old ways" as Mr. Gladstone, thought the book worth criticising and censuring, he bore eloquent testimony to the effect it was evidently destined to produce. Its influence has unquestionably been great. There are many people who owe to it their first acquaintance with modern religious thought. Numbers of the younger clergymen of the Establishment must have been profoundly moved by it, because the faith of an Anglican is a comparatively elastic thing compared with the rigidity of supernatural conceptions which distinguishes the Roman Catholic communion. It may even be true that these sporadic outbreaks of Ritualism, which are so seriously threatening to "trouble Israel's peace," owe no little of their force to the far-reaching effects of the new religious controversy. The Newcomes of to-day, like their prototype in the novel, may very well have come to the belief that there is no salvation from that besetting demon of reason and "intellectual pride," but in a religion of sensuousness and externalism which Sydney Smith, himself, of course, a clergyman, once contemptuously designated as "painted jackets and sanctified watering-pots". *Panem et Circenses*! Bread and games! Give them fumes of incense, blare and blaze of sounds and lights, and they may learn to forget that there ever was such a thing as a school of biblical criticism which has turned orthodoxy into a heresy against reason by telling the truth about the Bible.

Biblical inspiration being attenuated to almost vanishing point, there is nothing left but to appeal to the Church—not, indeed, to the Church of to-day, lost amid the mazes and intricacies of sects and schisms, but to that venerable fiction, "the undivided Church" of the first few centuries of our era, and thus brand religion with the stigma of retrogression by proclaiming it the only thing which is incapable of progress.

Not infrequently is a progressive movement attended at first by a partial reaction, and it is not at all unlikely that Ritualistic clergymen have been terrified into an increased reliance upon forms and rites by the disastrous effects produced upon many of their followers or fellow-churchmen by the new controversial methods of Mrs. Humphry Ward.

Now, what is this new controversy? It consists in the adoption of the handiest implement available to literary genius, namely, the novel, or fictional history, and by consummate critical and constructive skill, showing the disintegration of the old faiths and the building up of the new in the life of some representative man or woman. There is much more in such a novel than appears. First, there is the work of the scholar, of the man of research. He is like the miner who works underground and digs out of the hard earth that "gem of purest ray serene," the truth. Then comes the artist, just as cultured as the scholar, and only less learned, who polishes the gem and gives it its setting in pages of brilliant writing, and what is more important still, weaves it subtly into the daily life of some human being to whom it has been slowly and always painfully introduced. Or, to vary the metaphor, this new controversy is an inoculation performed by one who possesses a masterly acquaintance with the circulatory system of the spiritual anatomy, and is enabled thereby to describe with unerring accuracy the precise effects of the new ideal at every stage of its progress through the soul. You see before you the experiment of a new ideal, at first only suggested, then partially welcomed and even loved. Then the awful struggle in which no quarter can be given on either side, and the final victory of the truth. Such is the new controversy, the world of truth brought down to the world of life, the fertilising streams of knowledge turned by some strong, wise hand, into the narrow channel of an individual existence for the purification and recreation of life.

Naturally, the distinguished authoress turned her attention first to the Anglican Church, the most cultured and liberal of the Christian communities. Evangelical dissent cannot at present be said to be interesting, at any rate from the point of view we are considering to-day. It is destitute of the historic associations of Anglicanism, and has been, until very recently, identified with ideals little suggestive of the intellectual or the beautiful. It can scarcely be said to lend itself to effective dramatic or artistic treatment. I am by no means forgetful of George Eliot, but every one will see at a glance that the handling of the religious question by that incomparable genius is entirely different from that of Mrs. Ward in the books we are noticing. *Robert Elsmere* stands for a system of theology and faith. *Dinah Morris* speaks for herself; out of the abundance of a pure and beautiful heart her mouth speaks words of wondrous grace and truth.

Hence, having held up the mirror to the face of Anglicanism, our authoress has turned her attention to that older Church, so rich in memories of the past, with so unequalled a record in the service of humanity, and able even to-day to command the allegiance, the nominal allegiance at all events, of more than two hundred million beings. In *Helbeck of Bannisdale* we have the world and life of Roman Catholicism displayed with a minuteness and a precision which I should have thought scarcely possible to one not "of the household of the faith". It is, indeed, an ideal world, a world that belongs to the past, for the Helbecks have all but passed away. The *Time-Spirit* has been too much for them, and that beautiful old-world courtesy, that silent, shrinking piety which was nurtured on memories of martyr-ancestors who were broken on the rack for the ancient faith, and long years of isolation and the proud contempt of the world, is now, as some Catholics regretfully deplore, a thing of the past.

No one knows this better than Mrs. Ward, and she has, I conceive it, purposely chosen a type such as Helbeck, almost an impossible survival in our time, because she could not otherwise have made Catholicism interesting.[1] Nor could she have succeeded in pressing home her own rooted conviction of the hopelessness of any attempt at compromise between the new spirit of reason and life and that of the faith of saints and martyrs. The modern Catholic, who stultifies himself and vilifies his faith by apologetic articles in this or that secular review, in which he attempts to show that the Church which taught the inspiration of Genesis and condemned Galileo was all the time not untrue to the scientific conceptions of Copernicus and Darwin, is a very poor person in the eyes of many of us; and one thing is abundantly certain, that by no possibility could even Mrs. Ward have made him the hero of a novel. For a Helbeck, who has reckoned up the chances of life, and deliberately made his choice, casting in his lot wholly with an idealism for which the modern world has absolutely no sympathy, we can and do feel a deep respect. But for your ambidextrous apologist or theologian, the fellow who can make words bear double meanings, and even infallible oracles tell contradictory stories, we have nothing but contempt, because he is a trifler with truth.

And, now, we may turn to the book.

Mrs. Humphry Ward has long taught us to expect excellence, and in *Helbeck of Bannisdale* we are not disappointed. She does not work, indeed, on so large a canvas as in *Robert Elsmere*, nor do her materials allow her to be quite so interesting as in that masterpiece. At all events, that is my individual opinion. The atmosphere is very close throughout the book, and one has a feeling that the windows of that old, old house of Bannisdale have not been opened for centuries. One breathes a stifling air. Light and freedom come alone through that delightful creation, Laura Fountain, a creature you do not easily forget, with an instinct, rather than a reasoned conviction, of rational truth and liberty, a being of almost wild impulse, clever, though partially educated, but good to the heart's core. Altogether, a winsome, lovable girl, and tragic as was her end, one scarcely knows whether she was not happier in her fate, hurried hence on the swift waters of the river she had grown to love, than she ever could have been in her projected marriage with one to whom religion meant almost unmixed gloom. Doubtless Helbeck found consolation in it, but it was such as he was unable to allow others to share. Noble as we instinctively feel the man to be, tender as is the passion wherewith he envelops the object of his love, the shadow of the Cross is ever there. Forgotten in the first sweet hours of their mutual avowal, it soon reveals its sorrowful presence, and gradually deepens into such unutterable gloom that the broken-hearted girl is forced to surrender first love and then life to the inexorable exigencies of his old-world creed.

This, then, is the issue of the dramatic interest of the story, that the attempt to unite the living with the dead ends in the destruction of the living, in the breaking of hearts, in one case, even unto death. For the lives and loves of Helbeck and Laura must be regarded as allegories of the eternal truths which encompass us. It may seem a harsh, a needless thing to cloud the closing page with such sudden and unutterable woe. Why should not these two pass out of each other's lives, as do numberless others who realise the mistake of their projected union? There is no reason whatsoever save this, that all things whatsoever are written in *Helbeck of Bannisdale* are, like the history of Isaac and Ishmael, told as in an allegory. They are symbols of the gulf which separates the new life from the old, and they serve to convey the reasoned conviction of the distinguished authoress that the inspiration of the "Ages of Faith" is inadequate to the complex needs of the larger life of to-day.

These two unhappy beings illustrate that law of growth and progress which forbids the youth to indulge in the pleasures of the child, or the man to find his recreation in the pastimes of youth. And as with man, so with the race. There was a time when the world was full of Helbecks, an age when the religion of the Cross was the highest, holiest, known. But man, in his maturer years, has outgrown that, just as the Cross supplanted an idealism more imperfect than itself: and the proof of its inadequacy is seen to-day in the blaze of evidence supplied by the slow and inevitable decay of those peoples who were once its steadiest champions. Spain and Portugal are being numbered among the dead. Italy and France are making violent endeavours to escape their doom, by restricting the liberties of the official representatives of their legally established Church, because they instinctively feel that their dogmatics mean death to the peoples who live by them. Hence, the cry, *le cléricalisme, voila l'enemi!* in France, and the *libera chiesa in libero stato!* in Italy. The modern state, the modern man cannot live by the old ideals: the dead would strangle the living. And, therefore, Laura Fountain, the modern maiden, must die.

For, look at Alan Helbeck. He is a man who felt, who knew, himself to be an anachronism, a man who had realised so fully the genius of his religion, that he was thoroughly uncomfortable in the society of any who were alien to it. He saw none of his neighbours; once only he had been induced to attend a hunt ball. The doctrine, *Extra Ecclesiam nulla salus*, he adopted in all its rigidity. He fulfilled Newman's ideal to the very letter: he was "anxious about his soul". He never gave anything else a serious thought. To escape hell—that nameless terror which stirs the soul of man to its very depths, as Mrs. Ward very aptly quotes from Virgil on her title page—this was the purpose for which Helbeck of Bannisdale conceived he had been placed here by a beneficent God. And on the supposition that "Acheron" is a reality, Helbeck was absolutely right. If hell is indeed "open to Christians," and if the path to life be exceeding strait and narrow, our bounden duty, as men of common sense, would be to "go sell all we had and give to" orphanages, like the Squire of Bannisdale, and appease this gloomy God by a life of austerity and utter renunciation.

Why, then, do not all Christians turn Helbecks? Simply because for the very life of them they cannot believe in their own inspired eschatology. Verbally, of course, they assent to the whole code of immoralities connected with future retribution, but "a certain obstinate rationality" in them prevents their translating their faith into practice. Hence, the Catholics we meet are no more Helbecks than ourselves. They do not believe in emptying their houses for the sake of orphanages, fasting rigorously in Lent, abstaining from intercourse with their fellow-beings, or going about chanting, "Outside the Church no salvation". Quite the contrary. But the truth remains that Helbeck was true to the ideal, and because he was, it is possible to see a romance and a dignity in his life, not always observable in his modern co-religionists. Nobody has anything to say against *their* "version" of Christianity, because it is, to all intents and purposes, identical with the sane ideals supplied by modern thought. No French or Italian statesman would have one word to say against them, but they have a morbid dread of Helbecks. If the Helbeck ideal were multiplied indefinitely, it requires very little foresight to pronounce the gradual extinction of the commonwealth. A nation of men who were simply and seriously living so as to escape Hades would make a speedy end of the most prosperous community.

And yet this man had once lived, aye and loved. But his love was lawless, and when all was over, he is taken by a church dignitary in Belgium to witness the death of a bishop. The prelate, weak in body, but strong in faith, is vested in his pontifical robes, and makes an extraordinary impression upon the young layman by the fervour with which he makes his final profession of faith. While in the exaltation of spirit produced by this solemn scene, he is induced to attend a "retreat," or series of spiritual exercises, to be conducted by a Jesuit in a house of their Order. "Grace" had apparently not finally triumphed, because he was within measurable distance of expulsion owing to the indifference of his behaviour. However, the preacher took him seriously in hand, and after one more stirring appeal to absolute self-surrender to the Cross, or, in plain language, to turn his back on the common human life of men, Helbeck's conversion is finally effected, and from that day to the close of his life at Bannisdale, his one thought was the Cross and the safety of his soul.

He had been living this melancholy existence for a number of years, when Laura Fountain, the daughter of a Cambridge professor, and a member of the Ethical Society there (so we are told), broke in upon his life. Her father, as much for pity as for love, had married as his second wife the sister of Alan Helbeck, and during his life had apparently succeeded in teaching her something of the gospel of reason, because Augustina practically abandoned her creed. But on the death of her husband, it revived, and she experienced a longing to return to her old home. Of course, there was joy before the angels and her brother Alan at the penitent's return. Being absolutely dependent for her creature comforts on her step-daughter, there was nothing for it but for Laura to accompany the invalid, and prepare to spend some of her time in the house of a rigid professor of a religion which her father had taught her to despise.

The utmost skill is shown in the gradual transformation of their feeling, from one of pitiful condescension on the one side and undisguised revolt on the other, to sentiments of growing esteem and respect which ripen at length into a love which is tender and deep. The love scene which ensues on that early summer morning when Helbeck discovers the "wild pagan" girl, as he thought her, in a state bordering on exhaustion, after her long walk across country through half the night, is a very beautiful and touching one, and reveals all the mastery which the authoress commands of the language and mystery of the emotions. The image of the infidel child had stolen into the strong, stern man's heart, and, next to the master passion of his life, his sombre religion, completely dominated him. They become engaged, to the almost inexpressible scandal of the household, from the sour old housekeeper up to Father Bowles, with his "purring inanities"—a wonderful creation—and the courtly Father Leadham, a Jesuit and a Cambridge "convert". But Helbeck holds out, trusts bravely to "the intercession of saints" and the attractiveness of Catholic worship, and thus some days of unclouded sunshine enter into his dark and troublous life. Like the gentleman he is, he makes no attempt at proselytism, and gives his word that by no speech or act of others shall his future wife be molested.

They spend a few weeks at the sea, where Bannisdale and all it represents is forgotten. Laura has grown to love and lean upon this strong, resolute man. She enjoys an almost unique experience in triumphing over a life which had been believed to be inaccessible to woman's influence. But the sunshine is soon overcast. They are back again in that atmosphere of depression which Bannisdale exhales, and the agony begins. The poor girl sees the life from the inside, so to speak, and the hopelessness of it all dawns upon her like a desolation. Never could she bring herself to say and do the things she sees and hears about her; a voice she cannot still seems to rise from the depths of her being, defying her to go back on her past and forget the life and example of her father. "You dare not, you dare not," it kept saying to her. No, the system would hang like a pall of death between her and her love: she could never possess his heart. Half of it, more than half, would be given to that ideal of gloom he worshipped as the Cross, which he correctly interpreted as the essence of the Catholic teaching. When, finally, Helbeck stands by the account given of the life of the Jesuit saint, Francis Borgia, who cheerfully surrenders his wife, disposes of his eight little children and then goes off to Rome "to save his soul" by becoming a Jesuit, the cup is full. Her lover tells her the story of his own life, how he had been brought to his present ideals—a story of exceeding great pathos, which utterly overcomes the sensitive, shrinking girl by his side—but it was the end. Half-hysterically she falls into his arms, and Helbeck almost believes the great renunciation is to follow. "His heart beat with a happiness he had never known before." But he was never farther from the truth. "It would be a crime—a *crime* to marry him," the heart-broken girl sobbed, when she reached the privacy of her own room.

And so she turns her back on Bannisdale. But fate compels her to return. Her step-mother is dying, and Laura's presence is indispensable. Once again the old battle is renewed 'twixt love and creed, and in her anguish this child of the modern world resolves to force herself to submit that she may save her love. Father Leadham can, he *must*, convince her. Has he not convinced Protestant clergymen and other learned people? Why not a poor, untutored girl such as her? But it was never to be. She was afraid to lose her love, but there was something in her which conquered fear, and it reasserted itself at the last. "I told you to make me afraid," she had once said to Helbeck in one of their sweet moments of reconciliation, "but you can't! There is something in me that fears nothing, not even the breaking of both our hearts."

And so, with the awful inevitableness of a Greek tragedy, the action moves towards the closing doom. It is sad beyond words, and we are grateful for Mrs. Ward's noble reticence. "The tyrant river that she loved had received her, had taken life, and then had borne her on its swirl of waters, straight for that little creek where, once before, it had tossed a human prey upon the beach. There, beating against the gravelly bank, in a soft helplessness, her bright hair tangled among the drift of branch and leaf brought down by the storm, Helbeck found her."

He carried her home upon his breast, and at the last they laid her amongst the Westmoreland rocks and trees, in sight of the Bannisdale woods, in a sweet graveyard, high in the hills. The country folk came in great numbers, and Helbeck, more estranged than ever now, watched the mournful scene from afar.

Such is the tragedy of faith and love, which bequeathed to the already lonely and sorrowful man memories so unspeakably sad, and led this new Antigone to immolate herself in so awful a manner—"a blind witness to august things".

For us there remains but one question. Helbeck, it is plain, can never win Laura, but can Laura ever hope to win Helbeck?

One would have to answer with many distinctions. In the first place, much has been done already. The true Helbeck type is fast disappearing, buried or lost in inaccessible places like the fells of Westmoreland, or Breton castles, far from the highway of humanity's daily life. Had not Mrs. Ward reminded us of him, we should have almost forgotten his existence. The modern spirit, of which Laura is the type, has steadily eliminated the species.

Next, though Roman Catholicism occupies a far different position from that it held in the days when Yorkshire and Lancashire were plentifully studded with houses and homes such as Bannisdale, it must be remembered that the successors of the sixteenth century Helbecks are only *magni nomines umbra*. To the modern Catholic, religion is less than ever a life to be lived, a distinct type to be created; it is increasingly recognised merely as a creed to be believed. Helbeck of Bannisdale you could pick out of a crowd, but a congregation at the Oratory or Farm Street differs in nothing from one at St. Peter's, Eaton Square, or the smartest Congregational chapel. They all mingle indistinguishably in the "church parade" and are lost.

It is the victory of the "world" overcoming "faith".

The modern Catholic believes with the Church as against the world, in the importance of "orders" or the truth of transubstantiation and infallibility, but his life is with the world. Emphatically, his *conversation* is not in heaven. He is one of us. He is like Nicodemus, a disciple in secret, for various reasons, of which he is probably utterly unconscious. His Catholicism no more alienates him from modern life than Wallace's profound belief in phrenology puts him beyond the pale of science. His differences with the modern world are purely speculative, having little or no bearing on practical life, and therefore the world is content to take Catholicism at its own valuation. How far this is from Helbeck one can easily divine, but Laura has brought them leagues from that Westmoreland home of impossible ideals and all it symbolises.

At the same time, no one need look for the disappearance of that speculative system known as modern Catholicism. The type, the life indeed has gone, and gone for ever; but there will always be a "crowd which no man can number," who prefer to sit and submit to being up and doing for themselves. Reason and authority must ever continue to be the watchwords of the two great sections into which humanity is divided on the religious question. They must ever be contrasted as habits of mind, as sources whence faith arises. But it needs no exceptional discernment to see that the religion of the strenuous and progressive, the peoples who move the world and make its history, cannot by any possibility known to us be a religion of undiluted authority. As a man is, so are the gods he worships, for the gods are the ideal. Therefore the progressive nations who find it impossible to stand still, not to speak of looking back, will more and more recede from even the remnant of the Helbeck ideal which remains to us to-day, and find their inspiration in a religion which is advancing like themselves. What! science grow, knowledge increase, freedom advance, and religion only stagnate! Perish the thought! Our religion, like our knowledge, grows from day to day, because it is only through the deepening knowledge of the universe and of himself that man is enabled to rise to a proportionate knowledge of That of which all things are but transitory symbols. Creeds and systems, prisons of the infinite spirit of man, never can they befit the age in which the ideal of progress has entered, like an intoxication, into the soul. "The snare is broken and we are delivered." Woe to the man, woe to the people, who are content to sit or stand! Woe to them whose hope is in the dead past, and not in their living selves! Woe to the faith that has no better message for the eager, palpitating generations of to-day, than a bundle of parchments from the third or fourth century, or the impossible practices of an age when the life of the world stood still! They shall never inherit the earth. The new heaven, the better land, is reserved for the strenuous and the progressive alone, for "the kingdom of heaven suffereth violence, and the violent bear it away".

[1] The Rev. Father Clarke, of the Jesuit Society, in the *Nineteenth Century* of September, 1898, refuses to recognise Helbeck as true to the Catholic type. Certainly, he is not a modern Roman Catholic, and probably Mrs. Ward knows this as well as her critic. The question is, which conforms to type, the old or the modern English Catholic? Mr. Mivart's "liberal catholic" criticisms of Father Clarke in the October number of the same review are good, very good, reading.

XIV.

THE RELIGION OF TENNYSON.

Prophecy and poetry are the embodiment in artistic form of the abstract conceptions of the philosopher. As the philosopher thinks, so the prophet preaches, so the poet sings. Thinking, speaking, singing, are the three acts in the ascending scale of the soul's self-manifestation. Generally speaking, these high functions are not found in their perfection in one and the same soul; rarely do you meet with the spirit of the philosopher, prophet and poet incarnate in one mortal frame. Such enterprise is too great for all but the greatest, and amongst these may possibly be classed the poet-prophet of Israel, Isaiah, the writers of some of the Vedic hymns and Hebrew psalms, and Jesus of Nazara, whose soul was full of music, and whose thinking and preaching will probably fill the thoughts of man throughout all time.

The significance of philosophical and prophetic teaching in religion is a frequent subject of thought in our circles, and now the recent publication of Tennyson's life enables us to say something of the *Religio Poetae*—the idealism which inspired the soul of a nineteenth century poet.

The poet's name is not without significance and interest. It is a Greek word signifying "maker" or "creator"—*Poiêtês*. There is a philosophy in language however much we continue to ask, "What's in a name?" When those wonderful Greeks wished to express the thinker's art, they spoke of

Sophia or wisdom; when they heard the first preacher who told them of their innermost selves, they called him the *Prophêtês* or prophet, the man that speaketh forth as from an illimitable deep; and when they listened to the soul of music coming from the lips of a Homer or a Sappho, they called it by the most expressive name of all, "making" or "creation". The poet was a creator. And so he is if we come to think of it. Out of the materials supplied to him by the thinking of other intelligences, he weaves his song of joy and beauty which holds our senses as in a spell, and steeps our souls in ecstasy. He is a "reed," to use an expression of Tennyson himself, "through which all things blow to music". He is the creator of the ideal world *par excellence*; the keys of the Unseen are in his keeping.

We say that he transfigures the thoughts of other intelligences, that he turns his genius to the rhythmic expression of the towering fantasies of the philosopher. And he does. Poetry without thought would be a jingle—a word which, if we may trust the reviews, is a satisfactory account of much of the "minor" poetry of the day. If a man does not see somewhat deeper into himself and things than the average human being, never among the sacred band of lyric souls can he find a lasting place. Philosophy is the propaedeutic of poetry. But surely, it may be urged, the book of nature is open to every one, and a poet's soul may sing of that without any need of the philosopher's interpretation. Has not some of the sublimest verse been Nature poetry? True, but this undoubted fact only confirms our statement. When Wordsworth interprets nature in song, he is borrowing from a philosopher; he is reading the thoughts of an intelligence other than his own. He is revealing to you the innermost thoughts of that supreme Mind, who conceived the beautiful whole, and made it to be a thought of himself. The deepest thinker is he who thinks his thoughts into deeds. There is a First Philosopher as there is a First Poet or Maker, and because we are in our innermost selves of his kindred, we have the power to think his thoughts again, and create an ideal world which shall be the counterpart of his own. Men may be philosophers and poets because the First Poet and First Thinker is their Parent.

This is not mysticism, still less imagination, but the soberest of realities. In it you read the interpretation of the indisputable fact that the world's greatest poets were men of intensely religious feeling. They come so near to the Supreme Poet that their sense of the Infinite is extraordinarily developed. It is gravely questionable whether a man can be a great poet unless the influence of his great prototype be a power in his life; unless his religious instincts be reverently cultivated. A religious sense is needful to the highest flights. Go over the greatest names of the past and present and you will see how "the Over-soul" has been the truest source of inspiration. The unknown singers of the Vedic hymns, Homer, Sophocles, Virgil, Dante, Shakespeare, Milton, Goethe, Wordsworth, and in our days, Tennyson and Browning—in them all the religious sense, the instinct of communion with the unseen world, is a distinguishing mark and characteristic. A name here and there may be quoted on the other side, but as far as my memory serves me for the moment, it would appear on closer examination that such were exceptions only in appearance. An excess, not a defect, of reverential feeling is often the explanation of such non-manifestation of religious emotion as we may notice. With Goethe, they would appear to feel the presumption of individualising, the great Soul of the worlds by even so much as naming him.

Who dare name him, and who confess I believe him!

There is a reverent as well as an irreverent impatience of forms associated with the Formless and the Infinite; and because of it one never yet heard or read of a man truly great who had not the profoundest reverence for religion. But, however that may be, it is plain that we are justified in speaking of a poet's religion, and in discussing the religious conceptions which took shape in the soul of one of the two great poets of the Victorian era.

Five years ago Tennyson passed hence, "crossing the bar" on that tideless sea, still as the silent life which left its worn-out frame to "turn again home". So much as the great poet desired that the world should know of his own aspirations, his hopes and fears of the great Hereafter, has been given to us in his own sweet singing, and a memoir written by his son. It turns out that Tennyson was no exception to his noble order. Like all the great singers he was a man of faith—a man penetrated to his heart's core with the sense of the indestructible character of the religious instinct, and of man's deep need of communion with the Great Life which is within and beyond him— the Soul of souls whom men call God.

The significance of this fact is not to be lost upon reflective minds. In an age when positive science has made a progress which borders almost on the miraculous; when discoveries of the innermost secrets of nature, coupled with astounding combinations of her elements and forces, which supply us with the chemical contrivances and implements for further research surpassing the wildest dreams of astrologers and alchemists of old, there has been an unmistakable tendency to push the Divine agency farther and farther back in the chain of phenomenal causation, until it would appear that it had been finally thrust out of the world altogether. "I have swept the heavens with my telescope," said Lalande, "and I have not found your God." "The heavens are telling no more the glory of God," said Auguste Comte, "but that of Herschel and Laplace." Is it indeed so? The past has done all in its power to make it so, and Lalande and Comte represent the inevitable and natural reaction against the incredible puerilities, the stupid, obstinate opposition to all science not in conformity with the Nicene and Athanasian Creeds, or the fables incorporated in the Hebrew Cosmogony. But that past is past indeed, and never can come back again. The world returns no more to discarded ideals; the conception of theology as "queen of the sciences" is as hopelessly impossible in the civilised world as the Divine right of kings.

The result is that prophets and poets are "men of God" still, and notwithstanding Lalande and Comte, the heavens are not so dazzling as to quench for them the glory of a Diviner revelation which they scarce conceal. I frankly say that I had rather believe all the fables of the Talmud and the Koran than that the empty shadows of a vulgar superstition are all that lie beneath the stately verse of "In Memoriam," or the "Rabbi Ben Ezra" of Browning.

The religion of Tennyson is a perfume which fills much that he writes. It is a "spirit" which broods over many a song, but is incarnate, so to speak, in the elegy which immortalises the tomb of his lost friend. For Tennyson, the spirit of poetry is the spirit of religion—a blowing to music of the deepest thoughts of the philosopher. In "Merlin and the Gleam" we may read this as in an allegory:—

> Great the Master
> And sweet the magic,
> When o'er the valley
> In early summers,
> O'er the mountain,
> On human faces,
> And all around me
> Moving to melody
> Floated the gleam.

The spirit of poetry, which bade him follow on in spite of discouragement, touched all on which it hovered with a mystic light, "moving him to melody". It was the soul of religion, binding the spirit of man to nature and to "human faces" in themselves, and to the Supreme, in whom all is One.

But what is an allegory in the spirit of the gleam is a reality in the song of love, "passing the love of women," which he laid as the noblest offering ever yet made at the bier of a departed friend. The religion of Tennyson is there, but the poem must be carefully studied if its true inwardness is to be grasped. Isolating a few stanzas wherein the poet, alarmed and perplexed at the cruelties and terrors of Nature, her dark and circuitous ways, her astounding prodigality and wastefulness, lifts up in his helplessness "lame hands of faith," and falters where once he firmly trod, many writers have professed to see in Tennyson the expression of a reverent agnosticism. Such agnosticism we may all respect, for it is very different from the noisy, clamorous thing which, aping in name the humility of greater men, insists that the sense limitations imposed upon its own intelligence shall forthwith be erected into a dogma to be accepted as infallible by everybody else's intelligence. Be as reverent as Darwin in your agnosticism, as tolerant as Comte, we would say to such men, and there is much to commend in your teaching; but spare us the ridiculous spectacle of a handful of pamphleteers and minor essayists arraigning the sublimest philosophy ever known to the world, and consecrated by the homage of ninety out of every hundred thinkers who have ever approached its study, as a system erected upon a mirage—the image of a man's own personality distorted by its projection into the infinite. Tennyson himself once said that "the average Englishman's god was an immeasurable clergyman, and that not a few of them mistook their devil for their god", That may very well be, but the philosophers of the world who have built the house of wisdom are not "average Englishmen," and to describe their theism as the imagination of an immeasurable man—surpliced clergyman or otherwise—is a criticism, not of the philosophers, but of their would-be critics. *Non ragionian di lor, ma guarda e passa!*

But Tennyson was a passionately convinced theist. With that scrupulous voraciousness which, according to those who knew him most intimately, was his leading characteristic, he surveys nature not only with the reverent eye of a mystic, but with the exact vision of science, and faithfully reports what he sees—so faithfully, indeed, that he was hailed by Tyndall in, the sixties as "the poet of science". Loving truth, "by which no man yet was ever harmed," he does not hesitate to portray nature "red in tooth and claw with ravine shrieking against the creed" of a moral and beneficent power. And when no reconciliation is obvious he can but "faintly trust the larger hope" and point hence where possibly the discords of life will be resolved into a final harmony.

    What hope of answer or redress?
  Behind the veil, behind the veil!

But these facts, however unmistakable, are powerless to alter the main inevitable conclusion that beneficent power does rule the cosmos, though they may modify it provisionally, until a better insight into the workings of nature supplies us with a clue to the mystery's solution. He is a sorry philosopher indeed who will insist that nothing whatever can be known because everything cannot be known, that an established fact must be no fact because no explanation of it is forthcoming. Tennyson is not one of these thriftless people, and the "In Memoriam," read aright, leads one upward "upon the great world's altar-stairs that slope through darkness up to God".

The poem is a drama of life. It was not written at one time or one place, but over a path of some years. Those years and places are a symbol of the ever-changeful thoughts and moods of man who communes much with the world concealed behind the veil of sense. It is the vivid portraiture of the soul, its sorrows, doubts, anxieties, and aspirations; it tells of the eclipse as well as of the dawn and meridian of faith. In fact, it is Tennyson's own religious life which is the life of uncounted numbers in these latter times. Before the supreme sad experience, the sudden, and to him incomprehensible, death of Arthur Hallam, the poet had agnostic leanings. He did then veritably fail and "falter" before the questions of life and death which beset him. His long years of comparative poverty, "the eternal want of pence," his failure to attract any measure of attention, his long-delayed marriage as far off as ever, the *res angusta domi* which made his family dependent upon him, all conspired to shut out the vision of anything but an iron necessity controlling him and everything. Such lives are infinitely pathetic, and perhaps one had rather devote oneself to ministering to minds distressed like these than to any other form of charitable enterprise. Such souls have been wounded inexpressibly; they are sore to the most delicate touch, and gentle indeed must be the hand, and soft the voice, which would comfort stricken creatures like these. To think of such afflicted spirits is to recall the picture of the ideal servant of Jahveh, of whom Isaiah sings in words of unearthly beauty: "A bruised reed he shall not break and a smoking flax he shall not quench," for only by ministrations such as these can they be healed.

Strangely enough, as it would seem, it was the last and saddest experience of all, the blow which almost crushed his life, which brought the young soul back to health and strength. It was the hand of death, inopportunely touching the fairest and noblest thing he ever hoped to know, which helped him to see that—

    My own dim life should teach me this,
  That life shall live for evermore,
  Else earth is darkness at the core,
  And dust and ashes all that is.

The conception of such a life as that of his lost friend, annihilated with the vanishing of the touch of his hand and the sound of his voice, was plainly an impossible one, and if one remembers all the bright hopes, the extraordinarily brilliant future which, in the judgment of all who knew him, were buried with that young life, it is impossible to marvel at the change his death produced in the heart of his poet friend.

Now this temporary eclipse of faith is truthfully set forth in the poem, together with the manifold reasons which weigh at times so powerfully, even with the most devout minds, suggesting that the universe is not "righteous at heart". We all know them well, for we have felt them, and it is a comfort for us to be assured that minds more penetrating, consciences more sensitive, and emotions far deeper, have been enabled to withstand the shock which nature so rudely deals at our moral instincts, and to believe with a fervour and enthusiasm conquering all obstacles, that—

      Good
Will be the final goal of ill,
To pangs of nature, sins of will,
Defects of doubt, and taints of blood;
That nothing walks with aimless feet;
That not one life shall be destroyed,
Or cast as rubbish to the void,
When God hath made the pile complete.

It is "the heart-piercing, mind-bewildering" mystery of evil and pain which has quenched the light in many a sincere and fervent heart. But it is not for ever. Two things we may remember for our guidance amid all this weltering sea of sorrow and distress. First, it is not all nature. It is only a side of it; and if it is the most obvious, it is only because it is a breach of the order and beneficence so uniformly obtaining. And next, the holiest hearts, the spirits of the just made perfect on earth were not adversely influenced by it. In spite of it all, an elect spirit, such as Jesus of Nazara, could patiently endure a life of austerity, and meet a death of unspeakable anguish with a calmness and resignation seldom equalled and never surpassed. "Father, into thy hands I commend my spirit," is a serious rebuke to those who suffer so little and complain so loudly that the times are out of joint, the world as probably as not the work of malignity or indifference, and that he is no God who does not stretch forth an omnipotent hand to slay the accursed thing of evil where it stands. This is in very deed "the crying of an infant in the night". We forget when we utter these foolish things that we ourselves should be among the first to fall beneath that avenging hand.

And so with Tennyson. It was the visitation of evil in its most mournful shape—the cold hand of death that fell upon the brow of his beloved friend—which opened his eyes. His faith in goodness, in beneficent purpose, was restored. The cloud was lifted for evermore. He married. Wedded love, mystic symbol, sacramental image of a union higher still, came at length as an added blessing, after years of expectancy and disappointment. "When I wedded her the peace of God entered into my heart," he wrote. His cup was full; "out of the abundance of the heart the mouth speaketh," and therefore he sang that stately invocation, that sublime *Magnificat* which, we may well believe with his own most intimate friends, will endure while the lips of men frame the sounds of our English speech.

> Strong Son of God, immortal Love,
> Whom we, that have not seen Thy face,
> By faith, and faith alone, embrace,
> Believing where we cannot prove.
>
> Thou wilt not leave us in the dust:
> Thou madest man, he knows not why;

> He thinks he was not made to die;
> And Thou hast made him: Thou art just.

Thus were "the wild and wandering cries, confusions of a wasted youth" forgotten in the song of adoration, which is in reality the epilogue of the elegiac drama. We can almost imagine its coming after the closing glory of the bridal hymn which sings to its last note of God:—

> That God which ever lives and loves,
> One God, one law, one element,
> And one far-off Divine event,
> To which the whole creation moves.

A wedding on earth—that of his sister—is thus for him the symbol of that love eternal which moves all things: *Amor che tutto muove*, of Dante's peerless song. That light of love once seen anew he never lost. As life declined it grew in intensity: brighter and more reassuring than ever did it glow as the darkness of earth began to close round him. It was borne in upon him with a depth of conviction too deep for utterance that death was but a fact, like any other in our many-sided life, that it was but a momentary occurrence, in no wise impeding that progress of the individual spirit in that path which has been with philosophic accuracy described by the Hebrew psalmist as "the way everlasting". The most perfect prayer is that: "Lead me in the ever-lasting way," for it is the destiny of man to one day reach that journey's end; to be one day perfect; to be absolutely conformed in mind and will to that most sacred of realities—the moral law.

It was this new vision which dawned on his soul, when the face and form of his much-loved friend was taken away, and filled him with a profound calm as the inevitable hour drew near.

> I can no longer
> But die rejoicing,
> For through the magic
> Of Him, the Mighty,
> Who taught me in childhood
> There on the borders
> Of boundless ocean,
> And all but in Heaven,
> Hovers the gleam.

In the old days long past, when, tormented with doubts, embittered by disappointment, he would fain be rid of his burden, the voice of the Master kept ever repeating:—

"Follow the gleam".

And so he followed—followed it through life, over the wide earth, until the land's end was reached. But even then the Spirit did not forsake him. The "gleam" still shone like a star in the deepening sky, till it stood at length over the waters at the gates of the great bar that led out into the Infinite. And last of all, the "call," clear and unmistakable; and there sure enough, waiting beyond the bar, was the "Pilot," the Master of the gleam, "ready to receive the soul".[1]

---

[1] Jean Valjean's death in *Les Miserables*.

XV.

"THE UNKNOWN GOD."

    The God on whom I ever gaze,
  The God I never once behold;
  Above the cloud, beneath the clod,
  The Unknown God, the Unknown God."
     —WILLIAM WATSON.

One great function of poetry is to keep open the road which leads from the seen to the unseen world, and as the last echoes of this noble poem die away, it would seem as though a door had been opened in heaven and an unearthly vision had been revealed to our wondering eyes. It is as though some strange inspiration had fallen upon one suddenly, like that which the seer in the Apocalypse felt when he said, "And immediately I was in the spirit". The truth is we have been led into the invisible world, we have gained with the poet "a sense of God". The strange, undefinable attraction of the infinite is upon us.

Perhaps we have not yet learnt how strong that fascination is; how that it is not only the source of that inner light which we see reflected in the countenance of the philosopher and saint, but that it is powerful to arrest the attention of men who are for ever saying that no such reality exists, or, that even if it does, man need no more concern himself about it. Has he not the solid earth and the realm of sense? Why should he seek what is beyond it? *O caecas hominum mentes*! Man cannot help himself. Well does the ethic master say, "What is the use of affecting indifference towards that about which the mind of man never can be indifferent?" And why not? Because man came thence? There is that in us "which drew from out the boundless deep". In some incomprehensible way the infinite is in us, and we are therefore restless, dissatisfied ultimately with all that is not it. "The eye is not filled with sight nor the ear with hearing," for in us there is the capacity, and therefore, in our best moments, the yearning to see and hear something which sense can never give. Greater than all that is here, in silent moments, when the senses are tired and disappointment steals over us, the truth of the insignificance of things bursts upon us. "Man is but a reed, the feeblest thing in nature," says Pascal in the *Pensées*, "but he is a thinking reed. The universe need not mass its forces to accomplish his destruction. A breath, a drop of water may destroy him. But even though the world should fall and crush him he would still be more noble than his destroyer because he knows that he dies, but the advantage which the world possesses over him—of that the world knows nothing." And, therefore, the universe is nothing to him who is conscious that there is that in man which made all worlds and shall unmake them—the eternal Mind, one and identical throughout the realm of intelligence.

This is no dreaming, but an interpretation of man and nature necessitated by the undeniable facts of life. The finite does not exhaust man's capacities, it cannot even satisfy them. He was made for something vaster. He is ever seeking the boundless, the infinite. Hence the most positive, the most scientific of philosophers, Mr. Herbert Spencer, believes that there is one supreme emotion in man, utterly indestructible, the emotion of religion; and what is religion but the yearning I have described for communion, not with the world, vast and entrancing as it is; not with humanity, admirable, even worshipful in its highest estate; but with that which transcends them and all things, the enduring reality which men call Divine? Spencer and Emerson are at one. Nothing but the Infinite will ultimately satisfy man.

Such are the thoughts awakened by the music of this poet's song, which haunts one with a sense of the mystery of the illimitable. I do not read it as a confession of agnosticism, save in the sense in which all philosophers are ready to admit that our knowledge of the ultimate reality of existence is as mere ignorance compared with what we do not, and cannot, know of it. I read it rather as a profession of the higher theism, or, if you will, of the higher pantheism, for it is immaterial how far we go in maintaining the Divine immanence, provided we safeguard the sovereign fact of individuality and abstain from all confusion of the human personality and the Divine.

There is prevalent a most erroneous impression that the Divine immanence and personality are two irreconcilable conceptions, and that to assert that the All is a person or an individual is at once to limit its universality. Such is not the case, as an analysis of the conception of personality will show. The philosophic term "person" is utterly indifferent to the ideas of limitation or illimitation. Its essential significance, its distinguishing note, is that of self-sufficiency or self-subsistence, prescinding entirely from all considerations of limits or their absence. Thus a stone, a plant, a brick is an individual, because each is self-contained and is sufficient for the constitution of itself in being, and were they endowed with intelligence they would be further distinguished by the honorific title of *person.* Man is a *person,* because a subsistent, self-sufficing individual, furthermore endowed with reason. *A fortiori* is the All a person, because if the Supreme is not self-sufficing, then nothing or nobody is. Hence we have to point out in reply to the strictures of the opposite philosophic school that so far from infinitude being an obstacle to individuality or personality, the Infinite alone, in the strict sense of the word, can be called a person, because in the Infinite or the All alone is absolute self-sufficiency realised. From the very fact, then, of the omnipresence of the Divine, because—

> In my flesh his spirit doth flow
> Too near, too far for me to know;

because, to use Emerson's language, "God appears with all his parts in every moss and every cobweb," or Mr. Spencer's, which comes to identically the same thing, "All the forces operative in the universe are modes or manifestations of one Supreme and Infinite Energy"—because of these momentous facts we ascribe personality to the Infinite, with no detriment to its immanence, since of no other being could they by any possibility be true. Theist or pantheist, it matters very little by what name men call themselves so long as they do not imprison themselves within the walls of the false version of the philosophy of relativity, which binds them over to acknowledge nothing beyond their five external senses, to identify the unseen with the unknown, and thereby to stunt and ultimately to atrophy the sublime powers, transcending the insignificant senses we share with the animal world, as the sky towers above earth, whereby this noble poem of the "Unknown God" was given us by William Watson.

And here we may turn our attention to the poem itself, to see, if I do not misinterpret it, the evidences of that ethic creed, the doctrine of the sovereignty of the moral law, which we acknowledge as the only rightful basis of religious idealism.

In the first place, it is only amid the silence of the soul, when the voice of the senses is still, that we "gain a sense of God" at all. It is a vision of the mind—of mind knowing Mind, of soul transcending all distinctions and recognising itself. It is the sublime region of the higher unity into which subject and object are taken up and their distinction forgotten or lost. It is at night-fall, in sight of the awful pathway of the stars which, one would think, should fill man with a sense of his immeasurable littleness, it is then that he realises that this boundless splendour is nothing compared to him, for something more than a million worlds is with him, in the eternal Mind whence all this majestic vision rose.

> When, overarched by gorgeous night,
> I wave my trivial self away;
> When all I was to all men's sight
> Shares the erasure of the day;
> Then do I cast my cumbering load,
> Then do I gain a sense of God.

But of what God? for there are gods many and lords many. There is the known God, of whom the Western world has heard so much now these two thousand years, the God of the most ancient Hebrew Scriptures, themselves acclaimed as his unique and authentic revelation, the embodiment of absolute truth. That God has not been forgotten yet. Just now his temple is thronged with worshippers.[1] Ministers of religions in America, archbishops in Spain, are eager in their invocations, and if we may believe our newspapers, the Cardinal of Madrid guaranteed the harmlessness of American cannon and rifles to those who will implore his assistance through the intercession of saints. It is the war-cry of old: "*The Lord is a Man of War!*"

But the moral sense, the Divinity within, as contrasted with the Divinity in the skies, tells the poet that this old-world god is an idol, a glorified image of man in his "violent youth," a "giant shadow hailed Divine".

> Not him that with fantastic boasts
> A sombre people dreamed they knew;
> The mere barbaric God of Hosts

> That edged their sword and braced their thew:
> A God they pitted 'gainst a swarm
> Of neighbour gods less vast of arm.

He is well known, this "God of Hosts". Doubtless once he was the Divinity of the worlds that stream across our sky, subsequently transformed into the god of battles, who ranged himself on the side of his favourites, baffled their foes by super-human strategy or even knavery, the god of carnage and bloodshed, progenitor, in direct line, of him who afterwards was preached as the god of devil and hell. What has taught the poet, what has taught man to disavow such a Divinity?—

> A God like some imperious King,
>   Wroth, were his realm not duly awed;
> A God for ever hearkening
>   Unto his self-commanded laud;
> A God for ever jealous grown
> Of carven wood and graven stone.

No church, no official religion, no cleric or synod of ministers appears to have raised a hand to inaugurate the emancipation of the Western world from its degrading belief in a "God of Hosts". It is only now, during the last thirty or forty years, that stragglers here and there are coming into camp and making their submission to the "sovereignty of ethics," the supremacy of the moral law, which dooms to eternal death divinities such as Odin, Jahveh and Zeus. It is to the emancipation of the conscience of humanity from the paralysing guidance of the great ecclesiastical corporations of the past that we owe that famous band of scholars, who, antecedently convinced on moral grounds that such conceptions of the Divine were sheer profanities, set about an exhaustive study of the origins and text of the biblical literature, together with an equally painstaking research into the history of kindred religions, which has resulted in the vindication of the root doctrine of prophetic and ethical religion—the absolute and unlimited sovereignty of the moral law, and the consequent identification of morality with religion. They have made sacerdotal, sacrificial religion an impossibility to all who are at pains to inform themselves of the facts: they have banished for ever the presence of that—

>   God whose ghost in arch and aisle
>   Yet haunts his temple—and his tomb;
>   And follows in a little while
>   Odin and Zeus to equal doom;
>   A God of kindred seed and line;
>   Man's giant shadow hailed Divine.

And now there comes a stanza of haunting beauty, the ethic creed set to music, a pathetic pleading, a self-abasement, in the presence of the Immensities around us, and yet a passionate vindication of man's right to sit in judgment on an idol-god such as this!

>   O streaming worlds, O crowded sky!
>   O life, and mine own soul's abyss,
>   Myself am scarce so small that I
>   Should bow to Deity like this!
>   This my Begetter? This was what
>   Man in his violent youth begot.

The lesson of history and comparative religion could not be more perfectly summarised. The sovereignty of conscience could not be more masterfully asserted. Of old we learned that man was "made in the image of God," but now we see that the—

> God of our fathers, known of old—
> Lord of our far-flung battle-line—
>
> he to whom we still raise our supplicating cry—
>
> Lord God of Hosts, be with us yet,
> Lest we forget—lest we forget!—[2]

we know that he is made in the image of man. Unless a movement of retrogression sets in; unless we have to submit to a paralysis of moral stagnation, the day must inevitably come when the "Lord God of Hosts," "the Man of War," "the God of Victories," whom Spanish viceroys and captains are incessantly invoking in their proclamations, will be swept into oblivion with the curse of war which gave them birth. But that hour of retrogression and decay shall never sound for humanity. A nation here, a people there, may drop out of the ranks; the last remnant of empire may fall from their unworthy hands, but as I have faith in the eternal order, as I bow before the everlasting Power which makes for moral progress, I know that war has served its purpose amongst men, and that the day *must* come when it will be finally abolished as unworthy of rational beings. At any rate, the war-god is not he in whose image the perfected man was made, for—

> This was what
> Man in his violent youth begot.
>
> This god was made in the image of man.

And as the mist of the phantom deity floats aside, there dawns a fairer vision of the veritably Divine presence on the reverent soul of the poet. No eye of man hath ever beheld him: it is a vision of the spirit. And as the

www.ingramcontent.com/pod-product-compliance
Lightning Source LLC
Chambersburg PA
CBHW081617100526
44590CB00021B/3469